Island Volcano

Endpaper map based on surveys by J. Healy, E.F. Lloyd and Professor R. H. Clark.

Island Volcano

WHITE ISLAND, OR WHAKAARI, NEW ZEALAND

W. T. Parham

Collins

AUCKLAND & LONDON

First Published 1973
William Collins (New Zealand) Ltd.
P. O. Box No. 1, Auckland

© *1973 W. T. Parham*

Printed in Hong Kong by
Dai Nippon Printing Co. (International) Ltd.

Contents

Illustrations

(c) *denotes colour*

Map

Preface

About four o'clock one morning in Belize, British Honduras, a taxi called at the Fort George Hotel to take me the ten miles to the airport. In it I found there were already two young men, who turned out to be New Zealanders from the paper mill town of Kawerau, near my home at Whakatane, who were also on their way to Jamaica.

As if this almost incredible coincidence in such a tropical backwater as Central America, at an hour when most people were peacefully asleep, was not enough, one of my companions told me he had been in the audience at a talk I had given in New Zealand about White Island.

He and I, like many people who live in that pleasant district, could not be indifferent to the lure of the volcano, so often trailing a plume of steam across the sky to justify its pseudonym, "the weather vane of the Bay of Plenty." It may be enticing when set in the blue seas of summer, or menacing against a thundercloud, but one feels its presence even when it is invisible in mist.

It may have been this tendency to cloak itself from view which suggested to the Maori the name Whakaari, one translation of this having been given as "that which can be made visible," or the vanishing island. To the Maori this place is wreathed in legend as are few others. When Whakaari disappears from view its sulphurous smell is often noticeable in Whakatane.

Many people would gladly heed the volcano's beckoning call, but it seems that a visit was easier in the days, now long past, when the thin-funnelled little steamers served these waters. Mrs Du Pontet has recalled how, many years ago, it was usual practice for the day intervening between the Opotiki Agricultural Show and the Racing Club meeting to be devoted to a White Island excursion by a Northern Steam Ship vessel, the officers and crew entering into the holiday spirit of the trip.

My task of writing this book has been greatly simplified by the remarkable interest shown by many people who were in a position to assist in one way or another.

I wish to pay a wholehearted tribute to the staff of the Department of Scientific and Industrial Research and the New Zealand Geological Survey, whose excellent 1959 publication is obviously basic to any subsequent study on the subject.

Since Mr W.J.A. Thomson's records have been destroyed, I was extremely fortunate to enjoy the complete co-operation of the owner of White Island, my friend John R. Buttle, whose family papers provided a great deal of information which would otherwise have been unobtainable. Mr S.R. Mair kindly granted permission for the account by Captain Gilbert Mair, N.Z.C., of the sale of the island to be reprinted. Mr Charles O. Stewart readily allowed me to quote his father's version of the legend of Te Tahi.

By pure chance I made the acquaintance of Mrs H.R. Rosser, whose father, Mr Gatland Gilberd, lived on the island for some years. He acted initially as assistant to Ronald Kennedy, then the resident engineer, but later took charge of drilling, retorting sulphur and plant maintenance. This old gentleman was particularly charming and helpful, his intelligent and receptive mind not only furnishing me with much that was new, but also correcting impressions I had had to deduce from insufficient evidence.

Mr J.H. Much, of Imperial Chemical Industries Ltd., London, contributed completely new information as the result of a search at the Public Record Office. Mr George H. Duncan, chairman of the Tennant Consolidated group in England, also sent personal recollections.

I went to the island in charge of parties to carry out banding work on the Australasian gannet. Dr K.A. Wodzicki, Ph.D., and Mr P.A.S. Stein, the two leading workers in this field, guided the project. The latter devoted a lot of time to comparing

10

notes with me from his researches at Horuhoru, these discussions being valuable when I prepared the passages dealing with wildlife.

Finally I am bound to place on record the long and unstinted support so freely given to me by friends of many years standing in the Whakatane district, covering both work at the island and the preparation of this book. Messrs V.T. Davis and H.D. London, J.P. deserve special mention in this respect.

I

Mystery Island

Every summer the Bay of Plenty, as one of New Zealand's premier holiday playgrounds, welcomes not only many old friends but also new visitors lured there by the wealth of its attractions.

Most of these holidaymakers are content to enjoy the seemingly limitless stretches of sand around this great half-moon bay, so often fringed by some of the finest of scarlet flowered pohutukawas. As the newcomers hopefully cast their lines into the waves, push surf boards out to sea for yet another short, swooping ride back to the beach, or merely laze in the sun, their eyes are inevitably drawn to the distant and frequently empty horizon.

Those who choose the central or eastern sectors of this coast, however, have a distant view of a tantalising island of mystery which forms the pivot of the bay. From Ohope it looks rather like a humpbacked whale. How different it appears to the bystander on the shore at Te Araroa, who sees the island as a ruined tooth thrusting jagged and hollow from the sea.

This is White Island, the country's only active marine volcano, which has been widely credited as being the safety valve which protects the surrounding area from such catastrophes as the Taupo and Tarawera eruptions. Modern scientific opinion does not support this belief.

Many of the visitors who flock to Mount Maunganui, Whakatane and the other tourist resorts would gladly go to this place, at once both enticing and repelling, if they could, but this is where the difficulty arises. The island is so small, being only about a square mile in extent, and lies so far out to sea that a vessel can find very little shelter there if the weather should change, as it can with only the shortest of notice.

13

The Bay of Plenty has known so many ships come to grief that the Marine Department quite rightly sees to it that passengers are as well protected as regulations can ensure. In the event of one braving the passage, which can take quite a long time, there is no guarantee of being able to land upon arrival.

The spectacle of ocean swells bursting high on the rocky, cliff-bound coast would surely deter even the most foolhardy from making the attempt. Only in the calmest conditions is it possible for a dinghy to approach the beaches, consisting chiefly of huge boulders flung out of the volcano which have been worn round and smooth by the incessant surging of the sea.

Why should anyone want to go to a place which has proved itself to be both dangerous and inhospitable to man? There were those who went to the island never to return, disappearing so completely that even the manner of their fate is still unknown.

Basically, in many cases, the attraction was that boundless human curiosity which today takes voyagers to outer space, but there has generally been a more solid reason as well. The earliest was the most elemental of needs, food. The volcano has ever been a source of both fish and fowl.

The sea surrounding the satellite rock stacks which rise so impressively and vertically from the water is favoured by fish in both abundance and variety. The mainland coast has long been heavily populated by the Maoris, who always relied for much of their sustenance upon the harvest of the sea. Inshore supplies were not inexhaustible, and the outstanding size of the hapuka and other prizes of the deep at this more distant ground was ample reward for the effort of paddling heavy canoes on a round trip of sixty miles or more.

Today the waters of the Bay of Plenty are famous for big game fishing. When the whale was more plentiful than it is now, this largest of the world's mammals often passed between White Island and the nearest part of the mainland coast, on the eastern side of the bay. Not only does this creature figure in Maori legends as a rescuer of those marooned on the island by way of punishment, but the people of Te Kaha and the neighbouring villages went hunting in the style described in *Moby Dick*.

A derelict whaleboat and a few trypots for boiling down blubber are all that remain, but a dramatic and tragic story of this fishery has been told by Mr Thomas Thorne Seccombe. The son of a pioneer settler, he spent his boyhood at Oreti Point, overlooking White Island and Waihau Bay.

One day, when whales rounded Cape Runaway to follow their usual track, he saw six boats put out from nearby Rauko-kore. One of the school was a calf, and a harpooner had the idea that if it was attacked the rest would stay in the vicinity long enough for the Maoris to deal with them. The calf was killed, but with unexpected results. Its mother went for the boats one after another, smashing five of these to splinters. The sixth escaped, to pick up the only two survivors out of thirty men.

For centuries before Captain Cook introduced his famous pigs, the remaining protein needs of the Maori were satisfied mainly by birds. White Island was well able to provide such delicacies in quantity.

The kereru, or New Zealand wood pigeon, by far the best contribution to the table the forest could offer, did not live at the island. Trapping this bird in small numbers was, however, replaced by collecting of prey on such a wholesale scale that it could hardly be called hunting.

Every year many thousands of seabirds came to breed both above and below the surface of the ground wherever it was suitable. By November the nestlings were well-grown, plump and tender. In addition to being in prime condition they were completely helpless, having as yet no feathers to permit escape from an enemy.

Human predators came regularly to seize such easy prey. The hunters not only had both the birds and fish to save them the trouble of bringing food to the island for use while they worked, but also steam jets to serve as an alternative to the hangi for cooking. Water could be scarce, but was usually

15

enough for their needs, so it mattered little if bad weather delayed a return to the mainland.

With the coming of summer, supplies of fresh meat were unlikely to keep for very long, so a method of preserving the birds was devised whereby these were cooked and sealed in their own fat. Long afterwards sulphur workers on the island, lacking a refrigerator, used the same idea to keep joints received from the butcher.

There is a widespread tendency to think of the development of minerals in New Zealand as something new, but in fact more than a century ago the country relied for years upon gold as its chief export.

Although White Island is most unlikely to become a gold producer, one man who was supposed to know about such things suggested, apparently quite seriously, that it might be a source of diamonds. This is indeed an exciting prospect, but if there should be any precious stones these are, sad to say, so securely hidden that I have never been lucky enough to find any.

In places like Japan and Sicily volcanoes are expected to pay their way in addition to being scenic attractions. In these lands the peaks were traditionally producers of sulphur long before other and greater sources were discovered.

The average person is unlikely to have very much direct contact with sulphur, and may well wonder of what practical value it is in the modern world. Most people will no doubt have heard of it in now largely discarded medicinal preparations such as ointments, or the disagreeable end of that one-time scourge of the nursery, brimstone and treacle. It may even be thought of in a still more uninviting role as the fuel feeding the fires of hell.

If one looks a little more closely, however, a use with far greater potential comes to light, for the substance finds a place in what is probably the most widely used of all chemical fertilisers, superphosphate. Long before the white man took much practical interest in White Island the Maori recognised the manurial qualities of sulphur, collecting it from the crater to spread on mainland vegetable gardens.

16

Since New Zealand depends so heavily upon the produce of its farms, the outlook in the absence of superphosphate would be bleak indeed, but this is only the beginning of the matter. It has been claimed that sulphur, also coal, limestone and salt, are the basic building blocks of the chemical industry. The amount of sulphuric acid used by any country is at once an index both of its maturity and prosperity.

As a small nation, New Zealand still has a long way to go along the industrial road. It can, however, be proud of the success of the giant mills converting the flow of pine from some of the world's largest exotic forests into a variety of consumer goods in demand at home and overseas.

An essential first stage of the forest products industry is to convert the trees into woodpulp. This can be done by using huge stones to grind down logs into short stiff fibres called groundwood, but for many purposes these are of less value than what is known as chemical pulp. Here wood chips are dissolved to yield long flexible fibres, and sulphur comes into the picture once again since it is an essential element in the process.

It can readily be seen how indispensable the substance is to the country's well-being, for a large part of the export trade depends upon it. Imported supplies run into hundreds of thousands of tons, and as with steel and oil, the balance of payments position would obviously benefit if the mineral could be produced locally. At the time of writing mainland deposits near Taupo and at Rotokawa are being tested with this in view.

For half a century, between 1885 and 1935, men of vision believed that White Island could do much towards satisfying the needs of the country, which were of course far smaller than at present.

Any new enterprise must inevitably place a burden of responsibility upon its leaders, especially if it seeks to exploit an untried field. In this case men had to have an even more daring brand of courage, since not only their own and other people's money was at risk but also the very lives of employees at the island.

17

Were the mineral resources of the volcano enough to make working it worthwhile? If so, would the products be competitive in the market? Was it safe for men to live there? If their lives were not in actual danger, how would constantly breathing acid fumes affect their health? Nobody knew the answers to these questions, which were some of the mysteries to be unravelled only by bitter and costly experience.

There is yet a further hazard which besets the entrepreneur in a venture of this kind, that of public censure. If he plays boldly for big stakes and is successful, he will be acclaimed as a far-seeing pioneer in the vanguard of progress. But woe betide him if he fails. With the benefit of hindsight, lesser men will then condemn him for recklessly squandering the shareholders' hard-earned money in an obviously hare-brained scheme.

There were no doubt times when reflections such as these ran through the minds of the two men who were mainly concerned in attempts to found a thriving new industry on White Island.

Both of them were distinguished in other and widely differing fields. John Wilson was a judge, while the globe-trotting Major Mercer gained his field rank when serving with the Indian Army during World War I.

The law was not enough to absorb all of Wilson's energies, and to him must go the credit of first trying to produce both a fertiliser and sulphur. He intended to export some of the latter, and to use the rest as a feedstock for the manufacture of sulphuric acid. Wilson certainly did not lack determination, for with various associates he devoted fifteen years to the task.

Mercer's staying power was even more remarkable, for despite a variety of setbacks his efforts were spread over two decades. Even the utter destruction of both his staff and installations did not deter him, for he went on to secure financial backing on a large scale both in London and America for a still more ambitious venture.

One cannot but admire the dogged tenacity with which these two faced obstacles such as a lack of geothermal data, makeshift plant and difficulties with staff and transport. Although success did not come their way, it was certainly not for the want of trying.

They needed plenty of financial and moral courage to persist in such an enterprise. Their men, who worked at the island over long periods, were always in some degree of danger to life and limb, as was unhappily proved on more than one occasion.

During the early days of World War II I was living in London when the city suffered German bombing for 88 nights out of 89. It was a far from reassuring feeling to go to sleep at night not knowing whether one would ever wake to see the light of morning. Those who not only worked but also lived in the White Island crater before 1925 could seldom have been entirely free of this nagging doubt at the back of their minds with an active volcano for a near neighbour.

I have often been asked, "Is the place really dangerous?" There is no doubt that a lot of over-sensational stories have been told from time to time, and the record of fatalities cannot be denied. But it is equally certain that the moments of peril have been very widely spaced over the years.

Men have felt and seen the ground rising under their very feet, while an eruption started in complete silence within a few yards of a scientific party in 1966. It is quite a common experience to have to run to escape steam charged with acid fumes when the wind changes direction. The loose and brittle surface on steep slopes can cause climbing accidents.

It could reasonably be said that while acute danger may be only an occasional menace, anyone ashore at the volcano should be extremely careful and wary at all times.

In an age when the sheer boredom and frustration of city life drives vandals to acts of senseless destruction, this spice of danger is far from being the least of the island's lure, though many who go there might be reluctant to admit it. This attraction is, however, usually only incidental to visits made for other purposes.

Men are still drawn to the island by the motive of profit,

though the gain they now seek is no longer monetary but the more enlightened one of widening our knowledge. This can occasionally suggest a role very far removed from the everyday New Zealand scene, as in the case of a visiting American associated with the United States space exploration programme. He considered the desolation of the crater to be so similar to surface conditions on the moon that it could well serve as a training area for astronauts.

Such a proposal is, of course, an idle one, but the volcano none the less remains a fertile source of enquiry for several sciences, notably botany, geology and zoology. It has attracted so many eminent specialists in these and other fields over the last sixty years that one might suppose all its secrets would by now have been revealed.

This is by no means so, for mysteries still abound on every side. What was the real reason why Captain Cook named the island as he did? What causes the sporadic growth of forest on the northern coast? Why do lakes appear and vanish for no apparent reason? Where is the big gypsum deposit reported by one mining engineer? Why does not the huge number of muttonbirds decline sharply when so few chicks are reared? These are but a small selection of the many unsolved riddles.

The answers to some may never be found, though scientists continue to probe. Expeditions often last for a week at a time, and although involving a fair amount of discomfort, at least provide a welcome break from routine for those who take part. On one occasion instruments were left working in the crater, these being coupled to a radio transmitter which relayed information to Whakatane.

When under heavy cloud the volcano, giving off masses of steam and ch~' ing gas, is so menacing that one can imagine few less inviting places. Yet one owner, the late Mr G.R. Buttle, once wrote, "Strange as it may seem, the island is unbelievably beautiful." How can such an apparent paradox be explained?

Bright sunshine can transform the appearance of most places from sombre to smiling, and nowhere is good weather more important than here. Under blue skies the grim bare scoria which covers so much of the surface gives place to such vistas as Buttle had in mind.

One of the most striking of these, at any time near the end of the year, greets the vessel passing the outlying craggy rock stacks as it approaches from the mainland. At both east and west ends of the island sheer cliffs confront the newcomer, and these are flanked by dazzling settings. The headland crests are snow-white with densely packed colonies of the Australasian gannet. The breeding grounds stand out in sharper relief because of the intense shade of green of a surrounding growth of the well-known ice-plant, flourishing in conditions very much to its liking.

This is no static set-piece, for not only a contingent of the gannets but also gulls and terns are constantly in the air on their countless errands, lending movement and sound to animate the impressive scene. In spite of the vibrant restlessness of the birds, their attachment to this strange home is one of the few unvarying features of a landscape more prone to change than most.

Linking these seabird colonies is something equally remarkable, a stretch of almost pure pohutukawa forest. This is one of the most baffling features of the island, for all the trees seem to be fairly young.

The seed of the pohutukawa normally germinates only if it falls on a favourable spot. How then could scores of acres of this finicky plant have grown so far from the mainland when much of the soil it occupies appears to be quite hostile to any form of vegetable life? Suffice it to say that the green canopy, dotted with scarlet blossom at this season, does much to soften the harsh outlines of the island.

Our passenger, by now impatient after a tedious voyage, will want to get ashore at Crater Bay, so that he will later be able to tell envious friends he has walked round inside the crater of an active volcano. If he comes from a land where thermal activity does not exist, this will make him out to be a daring, devil-may-care sort of fellow indeed upon his return home.

21

Island Volcano

There was a time when White Island could hold its own with the Grand Canyon in the poetic licence taken in naming its chief attractions. Arizona's Shiva's Temple or Wotan's Throne were matched by Lot's Wife, Schubert's Fairy or the Seven Dwarfs. Alas! The passage of time has borne these away, and in this more utilitarian age they have been replaced by nothing more imaginative than Big John or Noisy Nellie, though humour in some cases has not been entirely lacking.

One cannot guess what the volcano may have to show this stranger, because the scene changes so constantly. Only one thing is certain. Nowhere else in the country will he be able to gaze upon a series of fascinating thermal outcrops and yet, whenever his eyes stray back along the path he has followed, there will be the blue sea lapping into the very edge of the crater where its curtain wall has been breached.

He will most probably fall victim to the oddest of all the island's attributes, its uncanny fascination for every visitor. During the years when I organised banding parties to work there nobody ever refused to join me, and, given the opportunity, members of the party were only too glad to return again and again.

Yet the volcano is as hostile to man as it is to plant life. The castaway who struggled ashore here with nothing but the clothes he stood up in would, at certain seasons of the year, find survival difficult in the extreme. This hostility and the lure form a paradox as hard to explain as so much else about this island of mystery.

next page
White Island from the south. On the left the fault round the crater rim ends abruptly at the site of the 1914 landslip. The outflow from the acid stream discolours the sea in Crater Bay

II

"In The Beginning..."

"At 8 saw land which made like an island bearing west."
(31 October 1769)

"The land seen yesterday bearing west and which we now saw was an island bore SW [this should be NW] distant 8 leagues. I have named it White Island because as such it always appear'd to us."   (1 November 1769)

So wrote Lieutenant (later Captain) James Cook, R.N. in his journal aboard H.M.S. *Endeavour* after rounding East Cape. This active volcano, the first to be discovered by Europeans in New Zealand, was not recognised as such by Cook, it being apparently quiescent at the time.

At least he avoided jumping to the rather ludicrous conclusion of a later explorer, the Frenchman Dumont D'Urville, who in the corvette *L'Astrolabe* was following Cook's track. On 14 February 1827 he sighted White Island in the evening. It was obscured from view from time to time by what was believed to be smoke, though it was more probably steam. This, he concluded, was from the cooking fires of the natives.

When naming the island, Cook unwittingly started a controversy which has never been satisfactorily resolved. Even in the absence of steam, the light coloured sandy ash and scoria of the cone, combined with the gannet colonies on the southern benches, would be quite sufficient to justify the choice of the name. My old friend the late Bernard Sladden, an undoubted authority on the history of the Bay of Plenty, was convinced that this was the true explanation.

On the other hand, when observing the island from a distance by telescope and noting the light humpback shape with its offlying rock stacks, was Cook reminded of the chalk cliffs and

27

Needles of the Isle of Wight in far-off Britain? His master's mate, Richard Pickersgill, who for all his varied shortcomings was a skilled cartographer, prepared a chart for Mr (later Sir Joseph) Banks, perhaps the greatest scientist of his day, and certainly not one given to condoning errors. This map, now in the British Museum, shows the name as "I. of Wight".

Nor is this the only disputed item in the field of exploration. Just as no true African would admit the claim that David Livingstone discovered the Victoria Falls, so the Maori contends that the honour of finding, indeed even of creating, White Island rightly belongs to his legendary ancestor Maui:

> "The island is stated to have arisen from the deep after Mawe, the paternal deity of the New Zealand theogony, had first touched fire, when, taking up the new element with both hands, he was so greatly tormented by the insufferable pain that he instantly dived under water to assuage his agony, and in the place where he shook the fire from him arose Wakari."

A second legend, however, gives a somewhat different version of events:

> "A tradition that comes from the land of Tuhoe (the Urewera country) is rather upsetting to the theory of Maui and the origin of the burning island of Whakaari. It is here stated that Motuhora (Whale Island) and Whakaari (White Island) originated as peaks in the great Huiarau Range near Waikaremoana. Jealous of each other, these mountains rushed headlong towards the ocean, leaving behind them the tracks which now form respectively the valley of the Whakatane and the valley of the Tauranga or Te Waimana. Whakaari taking the latter route outstripped Motuhora and so occupied the commanding position on which it stands today."

The facts are rather less romantic. The island is a peak which breaks the surface of the sea after rising from a submarine platform ten miles long and five miles wide. The northernmost of New Zealand's active volcanoes, it is situated 37°31'S. latitude and 177°11'E. longitude. The area enclosed by the coastal survey is 580 acres, but since most of the land consists of steep slopes, its actual extent has been variously estimated between 660 and 800 acres.

Other pinnacles also rise from the underwater formation. The Volkner Rocks, precipitous lava plugs standing a few miles west of the island, were named in memory of the Rev Carl Sylvius Volkner, the Anglican missionary murdered at Opotiki in March, 1865 by fanatics of the Hauhau movement. These are also sometimes called the Needles.

The Club Rocks, lying close to the southern coast, have a happier connotation. At one period, when the island's mineral deposits were being mined, the workers lived in a small settlement among the pohutukawa trees overlooking the scattered gannet colonies at Ohauora. They noticed that while the mated birds nested there, some of the younger, non-breeding adults roosted on the offshore rock stacks, and so facetiously dubbed these islets the "Bachelor's Club." In the course of time the official name was adapted from this joke.

As is well-known, New Zealand's areas of fascinating geothermal activity are no more than a small segment of an immensely long seismic and volcanic belt which encircles the entire Pacific Ocean, and is one of the dominant features of world geology. A gigantic submarine canyon extends from the Tongan archipelago almost to New Zealand, the southern end of which is known as the Kermadec Trench, though since in some places this is six miles deep, it may be questioned whether such a description is entirely adequate. Parallel to this lies the White Island Trench which, although on a much smaller scale, reaches a depth of more than 4,000 feet at a point five miles east of the volcano.

A clearly defined fault line runs south-west from the island, on the course of which as it nears the mainland coast at Whakatane is a spot known locally as the "Bubbles", where large bubbles, probably of gas escaping from the sea bed, rise erratically from the depths looking rather like jellyfish swimming in the clear water. Whale Island, also of volcanic origin, still has a valley with steam vents hot enough to cook meals for muttonbirders.

Ashore, the fault continues southwards by way of the Whakatane and Rotorua-Taupo grabens to the cluster of volcanic peaks in the Tongariro National Park. Apart from tourist attractions in the Rotorua district, some of the better-known points associated with the feature include the geothermal steam fields of Kawerau, Waiotapu and Wairakei, and a string of active and dormant or extinct volcanoes, among which are Edgecumbe, Tarawera, Tauhara, Tongariro, Ngauruhoe and Ruapehu. The site of Lake Taupo itself was the scene of a prehistoric cataclysm on a scale fortunately unknown today, since it converted much of the central North Island into a wasteland for centuries.

The Maori, of course, observed this natural phenomenon long before the arrival of the white man, and the legend makers duly supplied an account of its origin. In a lecture on the geology of the Auckland province given by Dr Ferdinand von Hochstetter the story was attributed to "Te Heuheu, the great chief on the Taupo Lake," though the speaker did not specify which of the four men who bore that name during the first half of the nineteenth century was the raconteur:

"The great chief Ngatoro-i-rangi, after his arrival at Maketu at the time of the immigration of the Maoris from Hawaiki (he was the tohunga of the Arawa canoe), set off with his slave Ngauruhoe to visit the interior, and, in order to obtain a better view of the country, they ascended the highest peak of Tongariro. Here they suffered severely from cold, and the chief shouted to his sisters on Whakaari (White Island) to send him some fire. This they did. They sent on the sacred fire they had brought from Hawaiki by the taniwha Pupu and Te Haeata, through a subterranean passage to the top of Tongariro. The fire arrived just in time to save the life of the chief, but poor Ngauruhoe was dead when the chief turned to give him the fire. On this account

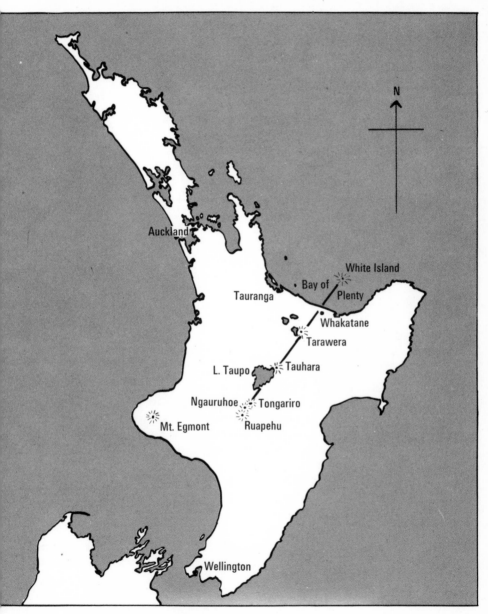

White Island – location

the hole through which the fire made its appearance — the active crater of Tongariro — is called to this day by the name of the slave Ngauruhoe; and the sacred fire still burns within the whole underground passage along which it was carried from Whakaari to Tongariro."

The name of the hero was also commemorated in Mt Ngatoro, the highest surviving point on what remains of the original cone of White Island.

When the need for fire was obviously so urgent one wonders why it should have been sent underground. It would also seem that this account of the origin of fire on the island conflicts with the legend of Maui. We may be inclined to smile at such a tale, but rare (and no doubt poor) is the nation without folklore.

It frequently represents a normal human attempt to rationalise an unusual occurrence, and only takes on an air of fantasy because the inventor lacked the scientific knowledge of later years. One may remember that, at the time of the Maori landfall on the New Zealand coast, the educated classes of Europe were firmly convinced the sun travelled round the earth, also that the planet was flat.

White Island figured in another version of the origin of the Maori settlement of the country:

"Ngahue from Hawaiki, a searcher after greenstone who, reaching Aotearoa in furtherance of his quest, touched at Tuhua (Mayor Island) and Whakaari. Finding White Island not to his liking, Ngahue did not tarry there, but continued his search southward where he was finally successful. It was after the return of Ngahue to his homeland that preparations were put in hand for what has become known as the Great Migration."

The Maori valued White Island (and still does) not only as a source of fire but of food. The surrounding seas yield a rich harvest:

32

"The weather vane of the Bay of Plenty"

"The silhouette of the launch against the greying sky . . ."

"Te Matawiwi (West Point) was one of the finest sights we saw"

" ... a muttonbird chick, covered with down ... "

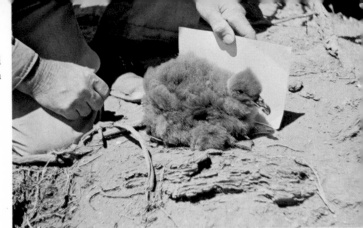

"One parent bird stood guard over the gannet chick"

"The broad bare ridge which terminates abruptly at Gannet Point"

"In the antarctic and sub-antarctic regions there is a natural drift of the waters from west to east, and a branch of this drift or current strikes northward along the shores of New Zealand. The remarkable abundance of minute forms of marine life in the ocean waters of the higher latitudes has long been recognised, and there can be no doubt that the plenitude of these forms in our own coastal regions is due to the northerly movement of the surface waters."

The heavy supply of plankton sustained a bounty of fish which in turn attracted both man and birds.

Since the island lay about thirty miles offshore, almost in the centre of the Bay of Plenty, seabirds found food and comparative freedom from human depredations. The Australasian gannet and the muttonbird nested on the outer slopes of the volcano in their thousands. While the breeding pairs were usually unmolested, Maori canoes converged on the nesting grounds when the chicks, though well-grown, were still unfledged and so could not fly away to escape the hunters. The young petrels were killed, plucked and preserved in their own fat, a somewhat unappetising delicacy to the average European taste but no doubt, like so many dishes, quite acceptable if one has been introduced to it early in life.

Food was also one of the area's main attractions to the early white men. Having failed to reprovision *Endeavour* at his landfall, Poverty Bay, Cook followed the coastline hoping for better luck later on. In the event he was able to satisfy his needs from the Bay of Plenty Maoris. The Rev Henry Williams, a naval officer turned missionary, also came here from the Bay of Islands in the 60-ton *Herald* accompanied by his brother William and Richard Davis. After collecting a cargo of food from Tauranga they sailed to White Island, and landed there on 1 December 1826.

Williams described the scene:

"We walked round the crater, which presented an awful sight. Its surface was nearly on a level with the sea. One of its sides having fallen in, we had easy access. Steam and

33

smoke were issuing from all parts of the island and to the very summit. There were several small lakes of boiling substance, and on the right a large body of smoke with the utmost fury rose up from the regions below. We examined this awful sight as minutely as we dared but from the intolerable stench of brimstone and the lightness of the surface over which we had to pass, we deemed it not prudent to remain long, fearing suffocation from the one or precipitation into some boiling cavity from the other. As the whole island was composed of sulphur, being blackened with the smoke gave it a ghastly appearance."

Gilbert Mair, the sailing master of the *Herald*, apparently stayed on board. He wrote later:

"It would be impossible for any person to remain on this island for any great length of time (say a few hours) as the smell of sulphur is exceedingly strong."

Mair should have been less dogmatic in his opinions, for men afterwards measured the time they spent there not in hours but in years. He fell into the same error as his friend Williams, for he added that sulphur existed on White Island "in vast quantities", another precariously based assumption which was to be frequently echoed in the future.

Although Williams and his companions were the first white men known to have landed on the island, it had been viewed from afar by that earlier trailblazer the Rev Samuel Marsden on 21 July 1820. He recorded in his journal:

"When we reached the high hills that overlook Towrangha, which lies about a mile distant below them, I sat down on the summit of one of the highest to take a view of the ocean, the islands in sight, and the mainland around. The prospect from this height is truly grand. I observed one of the islands distant fifteen leagues from the main sending up immense columns of smoke."

D'Urville, upon his arrival in Sydney en route for New

Zealand, naturally got in touch with Marsden, who was then living in New South Wales, for information. Among other things, the latter recounted his hilltop survey of the Bay of Plenty, mentioning an island volcano as being forty miles out to sea. He now claimed to have distinctly seen it sending up not only smoke but flames as well.

After first sighting White Island, the Frenchman had little chance to do anything further until 17 February, for he spent the intervening days battling for life with one of the worst storms encountered on the voyage, his peace of mind being further troubled by the knowledge that he was uncomfortably close to a lee shore.

The weather then cleared, and despite the fact that he had already seen the volcano smoking he spent a good deal of time in the morning looking for it. The possibility that it might be White Island evidently did not occur to him, even though this was the only one anywhere near the position Marsden had indicated. He concluded the missionary's story was merely some rumour based on accounts given him by savages, even though Marsden had seen the place with his own eyes and said so.

A month later *L'Astrolabe* reached the Bay of Islands, where D'Urville was told that the volcano and Pouhia-i-Wakadi (Whakaari) were one and the same. It is difficult to escape the feeling that this officer, destined to rise to the rank of admiral, had not perhaps found his milieu as an explorer.

Captain Byron Drury, who carried out hydrographic work in H.M.S. *Pandora* during the mid-century years, wrote of his visit more than two decades after Williams:

"White Island is about three miles in circumference and 860 feet high; the base of the crater is 1½ miles in circuit, and level with the sea; in the centre is a boiling spring about 100 yards in circumference, sending volumes of steam full 2,000 feet high in calm weather; round the edges of the crater are numerous small geysers, sounding like so many high-pressure engines, and emitting steam with such velocity that a stone thrown into the vortex would immediately be shot into the air. Here and there are lakes of sulphurous water dormant; but the whole island is heated so as to make it difficult to walk; from the edges of the crater, the scene below is only to be compared to a well-dressed meadow of gorgeous green, with meandering streams feeding the boiling cauldron; but on approaching it is found to be the purest crystalline sulphur. No animal or insect breathes on the island, scarcely a limpet on the stones, and 200 fathoms will hardly reach the bottom within half a mile of its shores.''

His comment on the absence of wildlife leads one to suppose that he was working at the island during the winter when the seabirds would have deserted their extensive breeding grounds. The depth of guano is, at the gannetries, ample evidence that birdlife has been established over a very long period. The deposits were at one time stated to be forty feet thick, though from observation of the natural contours of the land this was almost certainly an exaggeration. Such colonies overseas date back to the Middle Ages. In the fossil record the gannet is known to have existed at least forty million years ago.

Drury could be forgiven for failing to detect the presence of the small, shy Maori rat, first reported in 1892 but almost certainly there at a much earlier date. It is thought to have been brought to the country by the Moriois well before the arrival of the main body of the Maoris about 1350.

It is worth noting the strength of the impressions the appearance of the island made upon these early visitors. The missionary was seeing a convincing replica of the hell which was often in his thoughts by virtue of his calling. "A well-dressed meadow of gorgeous green" is surely a phrase of poetic quality hardly to be expected from such a matter-of-fact person as the average Victorian sea-captain.

The third recorded landing before 1864, by David Burn, produced the most vivid tribute yet to the scenic grandeur of the crater:

"The magnificent spectacle presented by the valley of

sulphur remains unforgettable to us. Its colours, its splendid green lake, its whistling steam jets, all these must be seen but can only be described with difficulty; surpassing all, and as it were, the central point of the whole, was a mineral water spring — looking like molten sulphur — in full activity, from which a column shining from afar in green and gold shot up into the burning hot air. The beauty of this spring surpassed all others, and the power with which it operated led us to suppose that the volcano is just now in a state of unusual activity. We approached closer only with the greatest caution, since the soil was in places soft and yielding and we could not tell in what kind of a sulphur pool a careless step might make us sink."

In August 1866 Edwin Davy, the Government Surveyor, visited the island and produced the first map. This was notable for showing the existence of not one but two lakes. The extent of the crater flooding varies continually, at times disappearing altogether. It is one of White Island's most intriguing features.

While ownership of the island was naturally claimed by the Maoris, Europeans were also taking an interest, so a map was needed. In Government circles the place was deemed to be Crown land.

There is a story that two unnamed English officers bought it from a Maori chief in 1861 for two hogsheads of rum, and went by canoe to inspect their property. They are said to have subsequently been killed during the Maori wars. Recalling the heavy officer casualties in the battle at Gate Pa near Tauranga in 1864, for instance, this account could possibly be true, but being so vague and unsubstantiated it seems most probable that it is no more than a garbled version of the acquisition of the island by Captain Hans Homman Falk (or Felk), generally known by his alias, Philip (or Hans) Tapsell.

In describing this purchase Captain Gilbert Mair, N.Z.C., son of the commander of the *Herald*, recounted a dramatic story of love and hate associated with the Maori owners of the island:

"Over a hundred years ago Puketapu pa (situated on the hills above Whakatane) was held by a noted ancestor of the Ngatiawa people named Rangitoheriri. He was succeeded by his son Te Rangitahia, who in his old age took to wife a woman of great rank and beauty, Kapua-te-Rangi by name. She was the Helen of Whakatane, and was beloved by Te Whakapakina, the son of Purahokino, the immediate ancestor of Te Hurinui and Te Kepa Tawhio.

"Now, Te Whakapakina was a wild youth of great physical attraction, and was wont to meet the fair Kapua in secret while her husband and the tribe were busy setting their nets in the bay near the western spit. But one night Te Rangitahia overheard Te Whakapakina proposing to Kapua that some dark night he should essay to climb the sheer cliff of the Sacred Hill (Puketapu) and carry her away.

"The jealous husband kept his own counsel, and made his plans accordingly. He strengthened the palisading and closed the waharoa, or gateway, of the fort, leaving only one small aperture resembling a modern cow-bail. To the top of the shaft, which worked on a pivot in a frame, he attached a stout rope.

"Night after night, rope in hand, he waited in grim silence till the moon had waned. At last after many alarms, his long vigil was rewarded by feeling the fatal rope in agitation.

"He immediately pulled on it with all his strength, and fastened the end to a stout post. Te Rangitahia then proceeded deliberately to inspect his 'catch', and found his rival, the gay young Te Whakapakina, in the agony of death through strangulation.

"Te Rangitahia kept a discreet silence as though nothing had happened, but the next morning a terrible cry arose from the women on discovering the body of their young Adonis. Purahokino, hearing the tumult and the mention of his son's name, seized his spear, and sallied forth from his pa at Kuhurua, above the Wairere waterfall, threatening to run the youth through the body for being the cause of so much domestic commotion.

"But on reaching the scene of the tragedy, and finding the body caught in the trap, he instantly divined the facts, and addressing his dead son he cried aloud:

"'My son, O my son! I feared that you had been detected in some petty act of pilfering food or other plebian chattels. Hence my determination to slay you. But I misjudged you. Your ancestors ever held that there were only two things a man should give his life for — land and women — and you have chosen to die for the greatest of these treasures. Had it been as I feared, I should have died from shame. But now I am unashamed.'

"But in spite of his assumed composure, Purahokino mourned sorely for Te Whakapakina, as David of old did for Absalom. He secretly sought the Whanau-a-te-Ehutu tribe, then living at Te Kaha, to avenge his son's death; whereupon they suddenly attacked Puketapu pa and slew Te Rangitahia.

"For this service they were rewarded by Purahokino bestowing upon them the famous Whakaari. This they held to the late 1830s, when Te Hurinui's grandfather Apanui and Te Kepa Toihau abrogated the cession to Whanau-a-te-Ehutu tribe and sold the island to the famous old Pakeha-Maori Philip Tapsell for two hogsheads of rum.

"Old Toihau was already noted for having broken the world's record by drinking a fathom of rum (six bottles) at a sitting, but he now went one better by drinking seven, which I believe still holds the record. Therefore his cask was soon empty; whereas Apanui, being extremely moderate in his libations, hid his hogshead under the sacred karaka trees at Pohaturoa Rock, trusting that the sanctity of the place would ensure its safety.

"But he had a rude awakening one dark night by discovering old Toihau and some boon companions carrying away the precious liquid in taha, or calabashes, leaving the cask empty. The robbers evidently believed the 36 O.P. rum was a sufficiently potent antidote against any infraction of tapu!"

Philip Tapsell was far from being the least colourful of the rich gallery of picturesque characters who have been associated with the island in one way or another. During his boyhood in Denmark he was an eye-witness of the capture of his country's fleet by the British at the Battle of Copenhagen in 1801 when Horatio Nelson, telescope to his blind eye, failed to see his admiral's signal of recall.

After years of adventure at sea when fire, mutinies, war and whaling provided endless adventure, he settled at Maketu as a flax trader on behalf of Jones and Walker of Sydney. The change in his mode of life was ill-starred, for he was ruined by incessant warfare among the cannibal tribes in whose midst he certainly lived dangerously. On one occasion he and his family had to flee by a roundabout route to sanctuary at Mokoia Island in Lake Rotorua. His eldest son, born at this time, was named Retreat Tapsell (Retireti Tapihana). His third Maori wife, Hine-i-Turama, was killed during the culminating engagement of the Waikato War at Orakau in 1864.

He successfully established his ownership of both White and Whale Islands, but failed to secure a third property at Matata. These claims were heard in 1868 when he was 89, and no doubt because of his great age title to White Island was granted on 27 June to his son Retireti and his daughter Katharine (Katerina), who was married to George Simpkins, a trader at Whakatane. The latter also owned a trading station on Whale Island, where Tapsell lived at one period after serious reverses. The number of family connections among those associated with the island's fairly short history is rather unusual.

There is no record that he ever made any use of White Island. His life in the Bay of Plenty was a long and courageous struggle to win a living against an endless series of obstacles of a most daunting kind. It is almost certain that even had he wished to do so he would not have been able to command the capital or credit on the scale required to exploit the island. This would necessarily have been far beyond the needs of his normal trading and shipbuilding ventures, nor was there any certainty that it would yield the quick profits of which he usually stood in somewhat pressing need.

Cargoes of sulphur are said to have been taken from the island for some years prior to 1868, but these were only small quantities collected by the Maoris or passing ship's captains who, not averse to filling empty spaces in their vessels, were ignorant of or indifferent to any owner's rights which may have existed. The Maoris are reputed to have used the mineral as a fertiliser on their vegetable gardens.

Retreat Tapsell and his sister did not retain possession for very long, since in the year following the Crown grant they transferred their joint interest to George Simpkins. Once again the capital needed to develop the property was too great for a trader in such a small provincial centre as Whakatane. Five years later, on 28 February 1874 he sold the place to Mr Justice (John Alexander) Wilson and William Kelly.

The change in ownership, involving city interests in Auckland for the first time, made little difference. Kelly disposed of his half share to John Mowbray on 3 November 1876, and the latter immediately resold to Frank Hugh Troup, no doubt turning himself a profit on the deal.

Troup's most lasting memorial was the bestowal of his name upon the great precipitous headland which separates Crater and Wilson Bays. Small quantities of sulphur ore were produced, but in a rather amateurish fashion. The shadow of serious exploitation did not fall upon the volcano until 1885.

III

Man Against the Mountain

On 30 March 1885 Henry James Johnson bought Troup's half share, and an Auckland syndicate was formed under Mr Justice Wilson's leadership, his son being among the participants. This new enterprise was styled the New Zealand Manure and Chemical Co., but while calling itself a company it still remained a partnership, with ownership of the island vested in Wilson and Johnson. It intended to produce both fertiliser and sulphur ore, the latter for export and also to be used in the manufacture of sulphuric "and other" acids.

A base on the mainland was necessary, the nearest port being Whakatane only thirty miles away, but since the river mouth served as the harbour it was obstructed by a bar which made entry for shipping difficult. The town was then a very small place, hemmed in by the great Rangitaiki swamp, considered to be the finest duck-shooting area in the country.

The choice fell upon Tauranga, although it was fifty-six miles from White Island. The extensive harbour gave complete shelter to shipping, while the hilly country lying behind the town was fairly well developed, providing a convenient market for fertiliser. A site was acquired at what came to be known as Sulphur Point on the shore of Tauranga Harbour. It was far from an ideal location, since to unload cargoes arriving from the island it was necessary to build a jetty 530 feet long to reach water deep enough for laden vessels to come alongside for working. It is possible the choice available to the syndicate was somewhat limited in view of the offensive nature of the works, entailing as it did the risk of acid fumes being discharged into the atmosphere.

At the island Te Awapuia (Crater Bay) was by far the most convenient point of entry to the crater flat, where minerals of economic importance produced by the constant thermal activity of the volcano were most likely to be found in quantity. While there is no record of where the staff accommodation was sited, it was almost certainly here, permitting the ready handling of shipments to and from Tauranga.

The mineral fertiliser, which was known as "White Island Manure", was obviously the easiest product to be initially placed on the market. This consisted of detritus from the volcano, claimed to be rich in sulphur. It required no more processing than quarrying, drying, crushing and bagging for sale.

A sample was entered in the Wellington Industrial Exhibition held in 1885, this being the first event of its kind to receive Government support. The exhibitor was awarded a silver medal for the product, which was judged to be the highest grade of chemical fertiliser at the show. At such an early date it may be that the competition in this class was not too severe.

Sulphur production would be a slower and more costly undertaking. Before making any substantial outlay on plant for acid manufacture it was essential to determine whether ore reserves were available in sufficient quantity to justify the expense. A drilling programme was therefore started under the supervision of Mr W. McCandlish (or McChandlish). This was considerably helped by the fact that at the time the lake was dry, and indeed this was the area selected as the most promising for the work. Fifteen bores were sunk, all of these being very shallow by modern standards, varying from 3 ft. 11 in. to 18 ft. 3 in., but two beds of sulphur three feet thick were proved. The engineer's calculations arrived at a figure of 20,954 tons of high quality ore, though this would obviously be of varying degrees of purity. Production commenced on a small scale, some 600–700 tons of crude sulphur being exported to Sydney in 1885.

In October the islanders were served notice that life in the crater of an active volcano was not without its hazards, for there was a sharp eruption:

"In the basin near the foot of a cliff over 800 ft. high a new opening has been made and jets of steam from it have thrown rocks of over a hundredweight right over the cliff."

Operations had to be suspended for some time until things quietened down again, but this incident was only the harbinger of a new outburst. On 10 June 1886 came one of the greatest volcanic cataclysms of recent times, the Tarawera eruption.

White Island was the nearest active volcano to Tarawera, and part of the same geological system:

> "The works on the island were abandoned in a great hurry by the men working there, owing to the great up-heaval. Afterwards it was said that this alarm was caused by the fact that volcanic dust was spread over the island from the mainland."

Whether the venture was considered too dangerous to the quarry workers, or if it was not paying its way is not known, but in any event it went into cold storage for some years.

It would seem Henry Johnson was in need of funds, for in 1891 he made over twenty-five per cent of his interest in White Island to the Bank of New Zealand. Five years later, two-thirds of what remained was passed to George Bentham Morris, though the latter transfer was reversed in 1897, when preparations were in train for reviving the project.

By 1898 memories of the Tarawera eruption twelve years before had faded to some extent, and the syndicate resumed operations. Sulphur ore was shipped in fair quantities:

1898	1,765 tons
1899	1,227 "
1900	1,692 "

This final effort was of no avail, for in 1901 only 143 tons were despatched, deliveries ceasing altogether in the following year. Wilson transferred his interest to the New Zealand Loan and Mercantile Agency, which may have advanced money for the business.

In July, 1907 Andrew Gray of Auckland bought up the fractional holdings of the Bank of New Zealand (now vested in the Assets Realisation Board), the N.Z. Loan and Mercantile Agency, and Johnson, so that for the first time since 1874 the island once again belonged to one man. Whatever Gray's intentions may have been when he bought the property, he does not appear to have made any effort to work the mineral deposits. On 17 October 1913 he sold it for $Can.20,000 to Archibald Allan Mercer and John Browne, who were acting on behalf of the White Island Sulphur Co. Ltd. of Vancouver.

So began Mercer's long and chequered association with White Island. He was then a young man, and was to serve in the Indian Army during World War I, when he attained the rank of major by the time he was demobilised. He was an Englishman with wealthy friends in London, also having connections in British Columbia, an area which provided (as it still does) attractive living conditions for retired British officers and their families.

He was a remarkable man on several counts, possessing both vision and organising ability while also being gifted with a particular flair for company promotion. John Buttle recalls that the Major normally carried a swordstick, and was reputed on occasion to have drawn the blade to emphasise his point of view. He also made something of a fetish of physical fitness, both for himself and others. At a time when youth clubs were far less widespread than today, he went to the personal expense of providing a gymnasium for the young men of Auckland, to whom he would give demonstrations of how the apparatus should be used. There is no doubt at all that he was deeply bitten by the White Island bug.

The new company did little with the property apart from a certain amount of prospecting. It then:

> ". . . for the purpose of financing the works and development of the island formed the present New Zealand Sulphur & Fertiliser Co. This is composed of Canadian capitalists, scarcely any shares being held in New Zealand. The capital of the company is £100,000, of which about £70,000 has been

issued. The vendors took their interests entirely in deferred shares."

The White Island Sulphur Co. therefore became a subsidiary of the new concern. Ownership of the island was never formally transferred out of its name.

Mr W.H. Willoughby, based in Auckland, was appointed to direct operations. A complex of wooden bungalow type buildings was erected on the flat between Troup Head and the south-eastern end of the crater rim, fronting on Crater Bay. This was known as the camp, and comprised a retort and boiler house equipped with three retorts, each with a capacity of four tons, also a laboratory and store. Living accommodation included the manager's house and office, kitchen and two bunk houses. The cost of the whole installation was put at £30,000.

An old friend of mine, long since retired, was once telling me of the none too prosperous days of his youth:

"In 1913 my mate and I saw an advertisement for men to go to work at White Island. We were tempted, for the money was good. Anyway, we never went, and later on we were very glad we didn't."

The company intended to concentrate on sulphur production, and set about draining the lake by means of a ditch to Crater Bay. It will be remembered that when drilling of this area had been carried out by the New Zealand Manure and Chemical Co. two promising seams had been found. Mr J.L. Stevens, chemist to the new company, outlined his views on the prospects:

"Since . . . 1885 the lake has at once risen and fallen, depositing on its bed the sulphur produced chemically from some of its constituents and that there has been further sulphur deposition in the original (1885) lake bed is proven by some measurements taken on approximately the same sites as McCandlish's borings where regular strata of a very pure sulphur (alternating with layers of sand and pumice-like material containing fine and globular sulphur) of a thickness varying from 1' to 5' in various parts and deepening towards the centre boiling pool (at present dry and converted into a blowhole) were found and these only tapped to a depth of 9'.

"Moreover, since the time of McCandlish's report the boiling lake shewn by him (the deposits on the bed of which were, of course, unreachable) has dried and shewn an enormous sulphur deposit at its edges to a depth of quite 30'. The lake bed deposits have been proved to extend back in all directions to the crater walls and the present flat site, under the hummocks of drift material that have accumulated. As the lake bed at present seems to have reached its maximum dryness, advantage should be taken of this favourable condition to extract as much of the rich sulphur deposits contained therein as possible."

If he was correct in his conclusions, the outlook appeared to be promising. The installations were finally completed and the plant commissioned in February, 1914.

Over many years the volcano seemed to frown upon the efforts of man to snatch wealth from its heart, but no such attempt was more ill-starred than this one. In May, only three months after work began, came the first fatality:

"A distressing accident occurred at White Island last week resulting in the death of John H. Williams, a married man, 32 years of age.

"He was employed by the White Island Sulphur Co. as a fireman, and was on duty on Monday 18th., when one of the large retorts used in extracting the sulphur suddenly burst under steam pressure, and he was terribly injured. The unfortunate man was scalded on his arms, hands, legs and face. He was treated for the burns, but succumbed at 11 p.m. on the following night. The body was brought to Opotiki by launch on the 25th. An inquest was opened last night, and adjourned until Thursday.

"Williams leaves a wife and two children, who reside in Upper Queen Street, Auckland."

Troup Head and Crater Bay as illustrated in the prospectus

Troup Head and Crater Bay in 1960

Noisy Nellie and Mt Gisborne from the crater rim

Shark Bay, the Pinnacles and Wilson Bay from Crater Ridge. Two people are in the centre of the picture

The accident was attributed to corrosion of the retort shell by acids released from the sulphur ore during the refining process. There was no alternative but to shut down the plant pending modification or replacement to prevent a repetition of the tragedy.

Firemen seemed to be a most unfortunate breed, for not long after the death of Williams his colleague Donald Pye was reported missing. Apart from his boots no trace of him was ever found. It was conjectured he had either met with an accident, whcih was all too likely if he was incautious when making his way about the crater flat, or that he had committed suicide. He was afterwards commemorated when the blowhole Big Donald was named after him.

The enterprise was in a difficult position. It was evident that the existing plant could not be used in its present state. This retorting process was normally employed in Japan, and gave the highest yield of refined sulphur. Stevens now recommended adapting the method followed in Sicily, whereby the dangerous acids would, as is too often the case with industrial wastes, be discharged into the atmosphere. This dated from very early times, the ore being filled into open cylindrical kilns, called calcaroni, covered over with spent ore, and then fired. The heat melted the sulphur, which was drained away to form blocks, but about a third of the mineral was lost by this method. The modification the chemist had in mind was probably on the lines of the Gill furnace which, whilst working on the same principle, used the combustion gases from one kiln to preheat the charge in another.

Whatever was done, it was obvious both time and money would be needed. The greater part of the subscribed capital had already been sunk in the venture, so it was decided to seek new money in London from the financiers whom Mercer knew. In the meantime a reduced staff was producing fertiliser on an experimental scale.

Although sulphur production had been the primary aim, Willoughby was carrying out field trials after "observing the totally unusual verdure of the pohutukawa growth at one side of the island", though he no doubt knew of the earlier "chemical manure". By June he had the results of these tests:

> "Central Nurseries,
> Auckland.

"The summary of the very complete experiments carried out by this firm on behalf of the New Zealand Sulphur and Fertiliser Co. has shown that the natural product of White Island, known as White Island Fertiliser, when applied in varying amounts to the soil, proved:-

(a) 200 lbs. per acre gave uniformly the best results.

(b) In every case a very large increase in yield.

(c) An entire absence of blight and disease in tomatoes, and potatoes in particular showing no signs of scab and the tops in a uniformly healthy condition throughout the period of growth. As a special test a number of tomato plants, which were almost destroyed by disease, were planted on 12 January. They made an immediate recovery and an exceptional crop was harvested.

14 June 1914.   Bennett, Green & Co. Ltd."

Later in the month Mr Mortimer F. Mieville, an expert sent by Mercer from England, arrived to examine and report upon the prospects of the undertaking.

He began by seeing for himself the effects of the fertiliser at experimental plots. It would seem that he was rather apt to jump to conclusions for, newly arrived in the country, he was "astonished at the extraordinary growth." By English standards the growth of vegetation in New Zealand can be remarkable even without the assistance of any manure.

He went on to the island for about nine days, during which time he claimed to have checked McCandlish's findings. Like Stevens, he considered the estimate of reserves to be far too low. He even felt his own calculation of available ore being equivalent to 40,000 tons of pure sulphur to be somewhat conservative.

Although no reference to his qualifications appeared in Mieville's subsequent report, he obviously had some knowledge of engineering. He came out against refining at the site, stressing the inevitable deterioration of plant in the fume-ridden air of the crater, the inadequacy of the water supplies and added cost of maintaining more than the staff required for quarrying in such a remote spot. As a mainland base he preferred Auckland to Tauranga, proposing the erection of a refinery alongside the water frontage already offered by the Auckland Harbour Board.

There was certainly some merit in this recommendation since a large proportion of any sulphur for sale would inevitably pass through the port. Machinery, pipelines, etc. would be free of atmospheric corrosion, with the further advantages of maintenance services and supplies close at hand. There would be a better choice of labour, and since the men could live at home accommodation and catering would be no concern of the employer.

Capital cost would have been the main objection to his scheme, since apart from the new plant envisaged, existing facilities both at the island and Tauranga must become redundant. These were likely to realise comparatively little in the event of a sale. Perhaps in view of having been sent so far he expected money to be plentiful, and gave little attention to this side of the affair. Another disadvantage he did not mention was the disposal of the large quantities of waste material from refining, such as sand and stones. At the island there was no difficulty, since this could be taken out of the factory and returned to the quarry, but its removal would have been a more expensive matter in Auckland.

Mieville further suggested that the company should buy at least two steamers, each capable of lifting 500 tons of ore. These could be filled by direct dumping into the holds from a cantilever truckway. He conceded the latter would be fairly costly to instal, but claimed it would pay for itself handsomely by reducing handling costs.

Rather optimistically, he believed there would be very few days in the year when bad weather might interfere with loading at Crater Bay. He was obliged to admit that Albert Mokomoko's launch, which in theory was supposed to maintain a weekly service from Opotiki, had sometimes been unable to call for three weeks.

The visitor was critical of the dirty condition of the camp, attributing this to a lack of proper supervision, but in every other respect his enthusiasm knew no bounds:

> "I have said nothing with reference to the possibilities of the existence of diamonds or other precious stones though microscopical examination of the sands, etc. . . show the customary accompaniments of precious stones."

It was really strange how many of the people connected with the mining ventures fell victim to unbridled optimism.

Mercer doubtless had his reasons when selecting Mieville for the job and going to the expense of sending him half way round the world. After this it was only to be expected that he would rely to at least a certain extent upon the report, even though he was certainly not naive enough to believe in it completely.

Unfortunately the document formed the basis for statements made when new companies sought to raise capital in the future. Mercer later held positions of responsibility, and has been criticised in this connection, but he could surely claim that the fault was not entirely his.

In the meantime, on the strength of optimism such as this, Mercer and Willoughby could confidently expect additional finance would soon become available. A new complication then arose, for early in August came the outbreak of what was to be known as the Great War, though at first few people realised that it would be waged on a global scale for more than four years.

Rather than wait until the results of the London negotiations were known, Willoughby decided to push ahead with fertiliser production on a commercial basis. He was quite satisfied with the results of the trials, and if he was to supply the market for the 1914–5 season there was no time to be lost.

There was the further point that in wartime a scarcity might well occur of fertilisers relying heavily on imported chemicals. With the provision of the necessary plant his own product, consisting entirely of local materials, would on the other hand probably be available in any quantity required. A reduction of competition could obviously help to establish a new brand more easily than might otherwise have been the case.

The island manager and most of his men had returned to Auckland, but left on 4 September to rejoin the small maintenance staff. They arrived on 7 September, and the next day were visited by Mokomoko making his weekly call.

He next entered Crater Bay at 6.30 p.m. on the following Tuesday:

"He steamed quite close in, but was unable to land as he had no dinghy. It was dark, and he noticed no change ashore. He remained off the shore until 11.30 p.m., making frequent signals, to which, however, he got no response. Then, assuming that the men were on the other side of the island, he returned to Opotiki, where on Wednesday last 16 September, he reported his non-success in attracting attention to the company's agent. The latter telegraphed to Mr Willoughby (in Auckland), who at once telegraphed back asking the agent to request Mokomoko to visit the island again as soon as possible.

"It was not until last Saturday morning that the pilot was able to go again to the island. He then found that a large portion of one of the cliffs had fallen away, forming a new hill, beneath which the camp and wharf had been completely buried. He saw no sign of life on the island."

Ten men were missing:

A. J.C. McKim, Manager	R. Lamb
A. Anderson	R. Waring
J. Byrne	H. Williams
W. J. Donovan	S.H. Young
L. Kelly	R. Walker

The last name appears to have been an alias, for the man was said to be really R.H. Chappell.

The inner walls of the crater are in places almost vertical, and consist largely of loose materials such as ash, breccias, mineral salts, sand and stones. It is evident that such steep slopes, in a situation exposed to heavy rainfall and earthquakes, must be highly unstable, and there was in fact a record of landslips noted by various observers. Raymond Buttle believed that the drainage of the lake by the sulphur workers led to the complete drying out of the friable structure, causing a large scale collapse. This seems unlikely since the lake bed had previously been dry from natural causes, in one case for as long as seven years, between 1886 and 1893, without exceptional movement of the cliff faces.

It is supposed that during the night of 10 September there occurred an avalanche on a scale unknown to the island in the modern history of the volcano, when a giant section of the western cliff slid down into the crater. While serious enough in itself, it is unlikely the debris from a simple landslip would have spread over the greater part of the flat, and since it occurred at the opposite extremity from the camp, the latter might have been unaffected.

The disturbance was, however, complicated by the presence of thermal activity. This has, during the last century, moved perceptibly westwards, and its advance could have undermined the wall. The bench left by the fall, standing 200–250 feet above the flat, has since become a well-defined area of fumaroles and larger steam vents. There is, of course, also the possibility that the slip could have been triggered off by an earth tremor, for these are common enough along the great fault line on which White Island stands.

When the cliff collapsed, it buried the big blowhole at its foot, the effect being, of course, the same as jamming a safety valve. The entrapped steam burst through the flat to form a new vent which later became known as Big Donald, and also escaped through fissures on the original site. The mud and steam thrown up set in train a lahar or mudflow which swept a mass of rubble inexorably down the flat to the sea at Crater and Wilson Bays. A similar outbreak from Mt Ruapehu in

1953 destroyed a section of the main Auckland-Wellington railway track at Tangiwai, with heavy loss of life when an express was wrecked.

Gatland Gilberd, who served as an engineer on the island in the years 1927–30, told me of a bore which was sunk at the junction of the landslip and the former lake bed. Although the drill penetrated to a depth of more than 300 feet, it found nothing but stones and other debris from the crater wall, the soft floor having been quite unable to withstand the great mass which fell upon it.

The plight of the doomed men was practically hopeless. Although higher ground on the far side of the flat from the camp, close to Shark Bay, was not affected since it had been bypassed by the lahar, they could not know this in the darkness and confusion. If they had been awakened by the turmoil, the flow could by then have cut them off from the safe area. A footpath connecting the works with the southern benches by way of the crater rim had not been formed at that time, and their immediate surroundings were steep cliffs, almost certainly unscaleable during an emergency at night.

The only real possibility of escape was by sea, weather permitting, which was always a matter of doubt at that season. Four craft were available, a dinghy and three surf boats, which were usually kept hauled out of the water on a concrete skid. If the men received sufficient warning of the calamity, it was conceivable there might have been time to get afloat.

The day after Mokomoko reported the disaster Sergt Ferguson took a police party of fifteen men from Opotiki to White Island, and spent six hours there searching for the missing workers:

> "A long trench was opened over the site where the men's huts stood, but nothing was discovered. The steaming hot debris forced the party to retire.
>
> "It is absolutely impossible under present circumstances to continue a systematic search, as the whole crater of the plateau is one steaming inferno. As showing the violence of the

55

eruption, stout piles embedded in 6 ft. concrete squares to carry the wharf were snapped clean off at the base. Fragments of the rowboats anchored at the jetty were found floating in the sea.''

The only survivor was the camp cat, which accorded its rescuers an unusually effusive welcome after its ordeal.

A second official party went to the island at the end of the month, led by Inspector Paul of the Mines Department. Surveys were made which disclosed 14 ft. of debris over the site of the manager's quarters, $7\frac{1}{2}$ ft. above the men's huts, and $4\frac{1}{2}$ ft. over the kitchen. The searchers dug a hole down to the previous surface level where the bunkhouses stood, but found no trace of these. The mud and rubble covered the boulder beach of Crater Bay to the margin of the tidewater. Loud detonations were frequent. On his return Paul fairly predictably recommended that no further work on the island should be permitted because of the danger to life.

The company had lost twelve men in seven months, although the island was occupied for but a part of even that short period. Every vestige of its plant and buildings had disappeared, and the only further wreckage found was a large quantity of flotsam washed up on the beach between Maketu and Tauranga late in September, consisting mainly of tramway sleepers and further remains of the shattered boats. After suffering this, his worst defeat, man abandoned the mountain to become once again what it had been for so long, a haven for nesting seabirds.

British pressure to increase food supplies to counter losses resulting from the German submarine campaign, also the need to reduce imports into New Zealand wherever possible because of the chronic shortage of shipping, may well have been the motives for a Government reappraisal of White Island's sulphur potential late in the war. The result was not encouraging, since it was decided that the likely quantity available was too small to be of much practical value.

After the 1914 debacle, the volcano remained in the possession of the dormant White Island Sulphur Co., for had it been saleable at all its disposal would probably have involved a heavy loss. On 31 May 1923 Mercer acquired title to it in his own name. Whether he paid cash or if he took it in settlement of money owing to him by the company is not known. It seems probable that the consideration may have been rather less than the $Can.20,000 which the property had cost in 1913, despite the severe inflation of money values during the decade.

Nobody could ever accuse him of not being an optimist, for although his initial foray had been so completely wiped out Mercer was planning a second attempt on the mountain. More than this, he intended to float a new company in British Columbia. Vancouver was then much smaller than it is today, and one might have supposed that investors in the White Island Sulphur Co. and its successor would still have bitter memories of their losses ten years earlier. The city could therefore have been thought to be a singularly unpromising venue in which to try to raise further capital for a distant will-o'-the-wisp when there were plenty of projects available in the local mining field offering less risk and better prospects of success.

This did not deter Mercer. He now realised that the previous selection of sulphur production as the immediate aim was perhaps a mistake, since not only was the provision of plant a more expensive proposition than for fertiliser, but there was also the real question as to whether ore reserves were sufficient to justify such an outlay. The extensive rupturing and burial of the crater floor during the upheaval of 1914 rendered the results of previous boring quite worthless. A new drilling programme would therefore have to be undertaken, in itself a fairly long and costly job. On the other hand there was no doubt at all concerning the quantity of material suitable for use as chemical manure, and the processing in this case was both cheaper and simpler, entailing no risk of a fatality such as had cost Williams his life.

While by no means discarding the eventual goal of sulphur, he judged it prudent to soft pedal that line for the time being, and consequently the next venture was dubbed the White Island Agricultural Chemical Co. Ltd. It had an address at Pender Street West, in the financial district of Vancouver, but this appears to have been the product of an office sharing arrangement with Arthur Coburn, the barrister who took charge of the legal side of forming the new company, in which he had an interest.

Mercer intended to keep control in a few hands, and effectively in his own. The authorised capital was $500,000 in ten dollar shares, of which he held 14,500. At least some, and possibly a fairly large part, of this $145,000 would have consisted of assets turned over to the company, such as the freeholds of the island and the mainland terminal at Tauranga. For his right-hand man he enlisted another former Indian Army officer, Major Martin Haddon Miles, who agreed to take up 8,500 shares, although these were paid up only to the extent of $60,000. A similar amount came from two Americans, Messrs Clark and Schneeloch, of Portland, Oregon.

A further $125,000 was raised in Canada and the United States on the security of $100 debenture bonds, convertible into shares at the holder's option, the Title and Trust Company of Portland acting as trustee. This capital was subscribed in comparatively small amounts by a number of people. Since they had no vote at meetings until they exercised the option to convert their existing security into shares at some as yet unspecified date in the future, the management of the company would be entirely in the hands of the large shareholders for some time to come, subject only to any action which may have been open to the trustee for the bondholders in the event of their interest payments falling into arrears. It will be noted that Mercer's share of the initial paid-up risk capital was greater than the other three holders combined, thus giving him a controlling interest.

He and Miles were not the only military men interested in exploiting the mineral deposits. In England on 18 October 1923 a new company was registered, White Island (NZ) Sulphur and Fertiliser Co., with an office at Salisbury House, London,

E.C.2. Maj.-Gen. E.D. Swinton and Major F.F. Trelawney were joined on the board of directors by a civil engineer, Mr R.J. Wellis-Jones, also two others who had connections with New Zealand, Messrs I.W. Raymond and T.E. Donne.

It would appear these gentlemen had been included in the 1914 group of London financiers and, as they went to the trouble of forming this company, were obviously still prepared to support the project. At this stage they went no further in the matter, being seemingly content to hold a watching brief while Mercer and Miles started operations on the spot.

The venture must clearly fall into two phases. It would first be necessary to organise transport to and from the island, recruit staff and establish living quarters, then commence production. Funds need be no more than adequate for these purposes, since any additional sums which could not be profitably employed at this stage would merely involve the burden of interest payments or represent excessive equity.

On the other hand, once production had started, it would be imperative to expand output as soon as possible to bring the enterprise to a level of profitable operation. This would certainly call for more money, with a reasonable prospect of seeing a return on the investment in a comparatively short time.

Having raised $390,000 in Canadian funds, which was quite a respectable sum in 1925, although part of it was represented by assets of perhaps doubtful value, the two ex-soldiers crossed the Pacific to New Zealand. They settled down at Tauranga which, like Vancouver Island, was favoured by former Service families. In this case, if they wanted an occupation, they seemed to like growing citrus fruit, but Mercer and his friend had sterner business in mind.

As a first essential at White Island an alternative camp site had to be found. For this they chose an area known as the southern benches. It lies between the steep outer slope of the volcanic cone and a narrow beach consisting of massive andesitic boulders. There is little doubt that this was the best spot for the purpose, with shade provided by the pohutukawa forest and the constant movement of seabirds during much of the year to give a feature of interest to a very isolated life.

While it is doubtful whether any part of the island could be described as safe, men would undoubtedly have a far better chance if they slept here rather than inside the crater. They would, of course, still run the risk of an eruption occurring while they were at work during the day, but at least this could then be seen and an effort made to avoid the danger. Unless an upheaval in the nature of an explosion took place close to where they were working, the extensive area of the crater flat would normally make it possible to run to a place out of harm's way.

The possibility of an explosive type of eruption has been canvassed at intervals since the famous Krakatoa cataclysm of 1883, the greatest explosion yet known to man, the dust from which encircled the globe, giving some memorable sunsets. The fact that the two are island volcanoes suggested this idea, though the level of thermal activity in the Asian archipelago is a good deal higher than in New Zealand. In both cases magma (molten rock) was near the surface, and an inrush of the sea appeared feasible. The crater flat of White Island does in fact rise and fall to a slight extent, but not sufficiently in recent times to permit ingress of the tide to the more active area at the foot of Mt Gisborne. During severe gales from the north or east seawater has been driven over the crater floor from Wilson Bay to Crater Bay, isolating Troup Head, but without significant results.

Near the eastern end of what became known as Bungalow Beach a bold flat-topped rock formed almost a natural wharf. A 25 ft. derrick and winch were erected on this so that materials (and if necessary men) could be lifted ashore for the camp. Because of the rapidity with which the weather can change in the Bay of Plenty, boats were also hoisted clear of the water for the night to obviate any risk of damage.

The standing timber at the site was too small and crooked in growth to be of much value for anything beyond fencing posts and firewood, so secondhand railway accommodation huts were bought for use as bunkhouses. These were each eleven feet by ten, and were joined together to provide a range of bedrooms. There was the further advantage that, being of sectional construction, these were convenient for shipping. Practically everything had to be taken to the island from Tauranga, transport being provided by the Northern Steam Ship Co.'s scows, equipped with both engine and sails. Later additions to the camp included the engineer's hut, dining room, recreation room, kitchen and cook's quarters. A radio shack did duty also as a post office, which opened for business on 1 August 1927. Two amateur radio operators, Ronald Kennedy who used the call sign ZL1FA and George West (ZL1AQ) maintained communication with the outside world.

Having made provision for the staff, Mercer and Miles could now turn their attention to production. While the men could go by boat from the camp landing to Crater Bay, this route was always at the mercy of the weather. As an alternative, therefore, a path was constructed which led across the south-eastern flank of the peak, requiring the bridging of a number of gullies. This steadily gained height until it crested the rim at a point close to Crater Bay, from which could be obtained one of the finest views in the country, over a vast seascape of the Bay of Plenty as well as of much of the island itself. The path then zig-zagged down the inside wall of the cone, taking advantage of a shelf which was once part of the crater floor of an earlier volcano, until it reached the flat.

Whenever the weather permitted, the men much preferred to go by sea. Gilberd told me that, working the winch of the camp derrick, he would first lower the larger boat into the water, and while that was taking on its complement of passengers, he launched the smaller craft. Running down into it he would start the outboard motor, and then try to overtake the other. After the race to Crater Bay the winner was often no more than a boat's length ahead.

Island operations at this period consisted purely of quarrying from the interior face of Troup Head. The distance from here to the shipping point at Crater Bay was no more than a matter of yards, which was spanned by a narrow gauge railway, or tramway as it was generally called. The only building was a wooden structure beside the track. The raw material for fertiliser production was then shipped to the works at Sulphur Point, Tauranga for breaking down in a bar mill, crushing to a reasonably fine grade, drying, sifting and bagging for sale.

By early 1926 Mercer and Miles could congratulate themselves upon having created a going concern, for sales of fertiliser were increasing, and the venture at least showed promise of being successful. In most businesses, however, it is usually easy to see how efficiency might be improved if the money were available for better facilities, and this was no exception to the rule.

To move material from the quarry to Tauranga meant handling four times, a costly process involving a lot of heavy work. The development visualised was to gather the quarried rock at a hopper from which it would be carried by pipe to a new breakwater cum wharf at Crater Bay for loading in bulk on the scow. When it arrived at the port jetty it would be unloaded by a similar pipeline direct into the building. The latter was not satisfactory, and it was proposed to erect a new concrete structure to house the fertiliser plant.

Portable equipment for excavating and removing guano from the gannet colonies was also required. The only work done so far towards sulphur production was the laying of further tramway track westward into the crater, which entailed making cuttings through the mounds left by the lahar. These disclosed a certain amount of ore thrown up from the former lake bed, but much more prospecting was essential to decide whether or not the reserves were large enough to support a refining plant. Quite apart from the question of expense, a suitable process would have to be devised to prevent any repetition of the earlier accident. Fairly low on the list of priorities came two steamers, by which the company hoped to become independent of hired transport.

There was certainly no shortage of desirable improvements; only the money was lacking. No dividend had yet been paid,

62

and even finding the interest due to the bondholders was not going to be easy until production and sales were substantially increased. The first stage was complete; now was the time to raise new capital.

The company was always vulnerable to local xenophobic criticism on the grounds that foreign capital would be taking profits out of the country, though these had yet to fructify. There was also the possibility of its becoming involved in double taxation problems in the future on account of the overseas domicile. Neither of these difficulties would be solved by an infusion of funds to the Canadian company from London.

On the other hand both could be eliminated and at the same time new money be raised by forming a New Zealand based company to acquire the business. The directors of White Island Agricultural Chemical Co. felt this to be the best course, and a new enterprise to be known as White Island Products was put in hand.

IV

White Island Products Ltd.

There was no doubt that the venture now entering its next phase was the most ambitious attempt yet to establish a viable industry. Mercer had gained a good deal of experience of the problems peculiar to the undertaking, and undoubtedly possessed such qualities of leadership as to eminently fit him to direct operations. Whatever his faults may have been, he was certainly not lacking in drive and initiative.

Efforts to work the deposits prior to 1913 had been handicapped by lack of finance on a scale large enough to ensure success if the mineral resources were present. It now seemed that this major hurdle at least was to be overcome, since not only would the new company be raising capital but if necessary it could also look to London for backing.

Technological development too had been fostered under the forcing-house conditions of World War I, particularly in the case of the internal combustion engine. This was far more mobile than steam power and, in the absence of an electricity supply, could save a great deal of labour in a setting where the humble wheelbarrow had previously been well to the fore.

By 1926 Mercer and Miles had a circle of friends and acquaintances in Auckland and Tauranga, but on the other hand as they were not well-known to the public generally, it was necessary to secure the confidence of prospective investors by inducing reputable local people to join them in heading the new company. The most distinguished of these gentlemen was Oliver Nicholson whose firm, Nicholson, Gribbin, Rogerson and Nicholson accepted an appointment as solicitors to White Island Products. In addition to his legal practice, he also served as a director of the Bank of New Zealand, the New Zealand Insurance Co. and Hancock & Co. His partner, Mr H.M.

Rogerson, told me that Nicholson was of an enterprising disposition, always willing to support any new venture he thought promising.

The farming interest had two representatives, one being Heathcote Beetham Williams, whose grandfather, the Rev. Henry Williams of the Church Missionary Society, had left the first account by a white man of a visit to the island. His family was well known from its outstanding contribution to the development of the colony in its infant days, and he had a sheep station at Hawkes Bay. The other farmer to join the provisional board was Charles Edward Macmillan, M.P. for Tauranga. The company was bound to have dealings with the Government from time to time, and it was obviously very useful to have a representative in Parliament.

The remaining director was George Henry Wilson. He, with a man named Canham, came to Auckland from Canada. They went into business as woolbrokers and hide and skin merchants. He may have known Mercer in Vancouver, but in any case the Canadian background would have given them something in common. Mr W. Crawford Young, an Auckland accountant, became the interim secretary.

So far so good; it was next desirable to enlist the help of someone well versed in the ways of the local capital market to take charge of the actual distribution of the shares to the public. Miles seems to have been acquainted with George Raymond Buttle, whose firm, G.A. Buttle & Co., undertook the task of organising the issue.

There was undoubtedly considerable enthusiasm for the venture among the members of this team. As Nicholson put it:

"I have carefully considered the position and am satisfied that winning and marketing the fertiliser product shows such a fine margin of profit as would assure a good dividend to shareholders derived from this product alone if demand therefore now in excess of supply continued, which there is apparently no reason to doubt will eventuate.

"As a result of my investigations I considered investment

in the new company was an attractive one with great possibilities, hence my consent to become a director and to personally invest capital therein. The owners inform me that they estimate the proposed plant will produce at least three thousand tons of fertiliser per month."

Buttle was equally keen when writing on behalf of his firm:

"There are always so many unforeseen difficulties in establishing new ventures that as a rule we stand aside until at least a measure of success has been actually demonstrated before advising our friends to invest. In the case of White Island Products Ltd., we have departed from our usual course, and while in no way overlooking the difficulties both known and unknown that will have to be met, have become so intrigued with this company's possibilities that we have assisted in the promotion of the company, and interested our friends in the venture."

Apart from old reports gathering dust in the files of the Mines Department, of the existence of which the new associates probably knew nothing, their opinions, as may be gathered from Nicholson's remarks, had to be based upon the information supplied to them by the vendor company. In this connection optimism had undoubtedly been allowed free rein, as exemplified by the claims which duly appeared in the prospectus:

"White Island fertiliser is a natural product, containing nearly 50 per cent elemental sulphur, a large percentage of soluble sulphates, free sulphuric acid, and a base of gypsum (sulphate of lime). The deposits of material on the island suitable for crushing and marketing are immense. The crater walls, which rise to a height of 1,000 feet, are composed almost entirely of this material, and they are sufficient without removing overburden to provide an enormous output for many years to come.

"The vendor company has proved the agricultural value of this fertiliser, and tangible evidence can be adduced respecting the same by the practical experience of farmers who have used it on their farms. . . . The value of the fertiliser has become so apparent to farmers and others that a demand has arisen for the same with which the vendor company cannot without additional plant possibly cope. The fertiliser can be produced and supplied at considerably less than other fertilisers now on the market, and then at a margin of profit which should give a good dividend to shareholders. . . ."

The method of estimating the sulphur content of a batch of material in the early days was rather rough and ready. A sample was weighed, placed on a long-handled shovel, and held over the fire in a blacksmith's forge. When the sulphur was thought to have completely burned off, the residue upon cooling was weighed again, the loss in weight being taken as the sulphur content. The fallacy was that the reduction in mass represented not only sulphur but also moisture, since the original matter was not pre-dried. Later on, when tests were made more scientifically, it was found the true sulphur figures were much below earlier estimates.

The prospectus continued:

"The deposits of guano are very extensive, and have not yet been fully prospected. The deposits prospected and tested to date by extensive pits and borings show over 500,000 cubic yards of varying grades of guano. As soon as a stable grade has been arrived at the company will be able to market a good quality of ruck and run guano at a price considerably less than imported guanos, which, owing to the ease with which the beds can be worked and the guano loaded aboard ships, should show a very fine margin of profit. . . .

"Other products of White Island are as follows:
(a) Ferrous oxide and ferrous sulphate. These are found pure or admixed with other materials throughout crater flat. These deposits have not been fully prospected, but their value is considerable.
(b) Gypsum. In pure form and in conjunction with sulphur, is found throughout the cliff area in the crater. The

deposits of pure gypsum are extensive, some of the seams running into hundreds of tons. Apart from its value as a component part of White Island fertiliser, it is saleable locally and very profitable.

(c) Barium, sodium, alum, have all been found in the crater but no efforts have so far been made to investigate the extent of these deposits."

The worst excesses of exaggeration were reserved for the passage dealing with the prospects for sulphur.

"The company understands that White Island contains the only deposit of high-grade sulphur of any magnitude in the Empire. The deposits of sulphur in the crater at White Island are vast. Sulphur in pure form exists at the westerly end of the crater in great quantities. These deposits, however, fade to insignificance when one begins to investigate the numerous deposits of high-grade sulphur ore, which runs from 50 per cent to 85 per cent and 90 per cent pure sulphur, and is found on opening up the cliffs surrounding the crater or in boring the crater flat. Certain active fumaroles at the western end of the crater are constantly ejecting molten sulphur, and the results of boring in crater flat (which has an extent of some 70 acres) has led the company's engineers to form the conclusion that the whole of the crater area at depth is a lake of molten sulphur. It is impossible to open up a square yard of crater flat without immediately uncovering deposits of rich sulphur ore.

"New Zealand alone imports upwards of 40,000 tons of sulphur from the United States of America annually. The major portion of this quantity is used in the manufacture of superphosphates. The market price of refined sulphur is approximately £5. 2. 6d. per ton thoughout the world, and it is perhaps the most readily saleable of any natural product.

"The sulphur of commerce is sold under a guarantee of 99.5 per cent of purity, free from arsenic and selenium. White Island sulphur is particularly easy to refine owing to its natural purity, and is always free from arsenic and selenium. It is proposed to erect a battery of brick-lined retorts on White Island capable of treating 200 tons per day. The cost of transportation of the ore to the retorts owing to the proximity of the deposits is very small, and will enable the company to profitably market a high grade of commercial sulphur at a price less than the same can be supplied at by foreign competition."

The above was written before Gilberd joined the company. We are not told who the unnamed engineers were or upon what evidence they reached their original conclusion, since for all their optimism McCandlish, Stevens and Mieville had not hinted at the existence of this golden underground lake. Some of the illustrations in the prospectus were in full colour, and it could well be said that the document was highly coloured in a double sense.

In fairness it must be added that it was very easy to be misled by appearances. One day Gilberd came upon a sizeable piece of apparently high-grade sulphur. When he had it tested it proved to be nothing but iron pyrites. He showed it to Mercer:

"That's an excellent sample of lake bed sulphur," said the Major.

"It's iron pyrites," returned the engineer.

Mercer and the manager, frankly incredulous, were not convinced until they saw it actually tested.

If the place was indeed such an El Dorado as was suggested, some querulous soul would be sure to want to know why it had not been exploited to the full years ago. To head off such enquiries the prospectus stated:

"Operations have been carried on for many years at White Island by various persons and companies, and considerable capital has been expended in connection therewith. These operations, however, have been mainly devoted in the direction of developing as a marketable commodity the enormous sulphur deposits of the island without particular regard to its other extremely valuable products.

"In the development of these sulphur deposits the owners of the island, prior to its acquisition by the vendor company, were confronted with difficulties as regards labour and shipping which, in conjunction with a volcanic disturbance at the island in 1914, led to a suspension for a time of their activities. . . . The vendor company has expended considerable money in its operations, and in the course of its development work has established the fact that White Island has products for which there is an unlimited profitable market, and has satisfactorily solved the labour and shipping problems with which their predecessors in title had been confronted."

Had the present more stringent legal requirements as to statements made in a prospectus then been in force the company might well have been called to account, since some of these claims were both extravagant and misleading in view of the inadequate amount of development work which had been carried out. The borings referred to were those of 1885 and 1914, which had no relation whatever to the post-lahar conditions. The sulphur was not always free from selenium, nor was it "particularly easy to refine." The plant which was subsequently installed was never able to raise purity above 96.5%.

Since in the case of products such as guano and gypsum there was no practical experience of either production or sale, the question of profitability could at this stage be no more than a matter of opinion, strongly influenced in this case by the desire to attract money. With any new venture there must necessarily be a certain amount of intelligent anticipation of future prospects, but it should at least be indicated as such rather than as a confident statement of apparently proved facts.

A number of the subsequent applications were for such miniscule allotments as ten or twenty shares, which were clearly made by people of very limited means who could ill afford to lose their money if things went wrong. Anyone reading the prospectus, and assuming its claims to be true, could hardly fail to believe the investment to be an attractive one. It was surely reasonable for those with no chance of verifying the statements to assume that the prominent people named as directors had satisfied themselves as to the soundness of the proposition. In fact the latter were little better informed than the general public.

The authorised capital was £250,000, of which 50,000 £1 shares were now offered on the local market, 5/– being payable on application, 5/– on allotment and the balance in calls of 2/6 at intervals of not less than three months. It was proposed to offer another 50,000 divided equally between Great Britain and Canada, but this intention was not carried out.

The vendor company was to be allotted 120,000 fully paid shares as the purchase price of the business. The sterling equivalent at that time of the $390,000 provided by the White Island Agricultural Chemical Co. was £78,000, so this meant a paper profit of £42,000, or nearly 54% on the vendor company's investment.

Mercer had it in mind to liquidate the White Island Agricultural Chemical Co. As an initial step the bondholders would be invited to convert their holdings into shares, with the inducement of a 10% bonus, so that the original $125,000 would become $137,500 (£27,500). The ordinary shareholders who had subscribed $265,000 (£53,000) would therefore divide £120,000 less £27,500, or £92,500, a gain of about 75% over two years. Whilst this would be reduced to some extent by debts such as outstanding bond interest, it was still a handsome return, even though any investment at White Island could only too aptly be termed capital at risk. The premium would doubtless have been claimed as payment for the goodwill of a going concern, but the truth was that the business was still very far from being firmly established.

The prospectus was circulated to brokerage firms throughout the country at the end of July, being favourably received since it was undoubtedly more elaborate than was usual at the time. Brokers generally were quite happy to accept a commission of 3¾% on any shares they were able to place, some anticipating the issue would soon be fully subscribed.

The new company agreed to pay a commission of 5% on

shares placed by the organising brokers, G.A. Buttle & Co.
The difference between the sum received from the company
and amounts paid out to other brokerage firms was to be shared
equally by G.A. Buttle & Co. and Miles.

The latter approached agricultural merchants, stock and
station agents and dairy factories with the dual objects of
inducing these concerns to take up shares and act as fertiliser
distributors. One of the most important of these contacts was
the New Zealand Co-operative Dairy Co. Ltd. of Hamilton.
At the time the directors were anxious to encourage the use of
low-cost fertilisers by their suppliers in order to boost milk
production. They sent representatives to inspect the production
facilities of White Island Products, which were considered to be
satisfactory. It was indicated that if a survey of the results on
farms using the product proved favourable, the dairy company
hoped to go further in the matter.

The quality of the White Island product as compared with
rival fertilisers was the really crucial question. A number of
users had written to the company in enthusiastic terms:

"I put 5 cwt. of your fertiliser to the acre in half a paddock
of 20 acres, and 5 cwt. of super on the other half of the paddock — yours beats the super out of sight."

"Re the mangolds and carrots grown in my paddock at
Opotiki, and recently exhibited at the Hamilton, Pukekohe
and Auckland shows. . . I am exceedingly pleased with the
results obtained. . . surpassing anything previously grown."

"I have ordered some of your fertiliser by wire after seeing
the effect on some early potatoes . . . . The results I saw today
are nothing short of extraordinary."

On the other hand, when I was once talking to Miss Violet
Macmillan, daughter of one of the directors, I asked her opinion
of its merits. She replied:

"I don't know about a fertiliser, but it was wonderful stuff
on garden paths. No weed would ever grow in it!"

This statement is well authenticated, since it is extremely

rare to find a weed in the crater from which the material came, while other forms of vegetation are completely absent.

Buttle, too, had his doubts about it:

"White Island Products Ltd. marketed a so-called fertiliser of ground-up country rock of deposit and sweetened this where necessary from the rich sulphur blocks to bring it up to the guaranteed 40% sulphur. In this raw state they claimed this fertiliser gave great results. . . . I thought the results, if any, came from the gypsum content, which must have been high."

Some users also were critical of its preparation for sale, considering that the moisture content should be lower and the particles more finely ground. Both of these points were obviously important to farmers in the days before aerial topdressing, when fertilisers were usually applied by drill.

As the White Island product had not been on the market for very long, the New Zealand Co-operative Dairy Co. wanted proof that it compared favourably with old-established favourites like basic slag and superphosphate. It appointed a committee of three experienced farmers, Messrs J. McCaw, J. Barugh and J.E. Makgill, who went on a tour of inspection between 26 and 28 October.

They visited Mr Floyd at Gate Pa, who showed them a paddock which looked well, though as it had been heavily dressed with basic slag for some years previously, it was difficult to determine the results of the two treatments. He believed the White Island product reduced the incidence of "cattle sickness". Since this trouble was afterwards found to be due to mineral deficiency in the soil, it is possible there may have been some substance for the farmer's view.

Mr Poole, farming poor land on the hills behind Tauranga, also believed his cows preferred grass dressed with White Island fertiliser, and the areas on which it had been used showed up well in contrast with other experimental plots. Mr White at Ohauiti and Mr Davidson at Ruatoki had only been on their farms for short periods, and knew little of the manurial history, whilst Mr Putt's property at Katikati had been heavily top-dressed before White Island fertiliser was applied. Potatoes which were inspected seemed to the committee to be growing tops at the expense of tubers.

The trio reported their conclusions:

"From what we have seen we believe that there is evidence enough to encourage full and carefully carried out trials of the products of White Island. The guano products should be of special value in conjunction with the other products. We were shown analyst's reports of the constituents of the manures now being offered, and noted that there is practically no phosphate of lime therein. There is a considerable proportion of sulphate of lime which has a manurial value and other constituents may have a beneficial action on some of our soils. This should be found by proper trials and proper recording of the results over a period of not less than three years. It is, we think, possible that the peculiar natural processes which go to produce these White Island manure products may provide certain forms of known chemical contents which may give results different from those usually expected from such constituents, and these may prove of distinct value on certain soils. We also consider that from the evidence given us it is important that full experimental trials should be made to determine whether the seeming improvement of stock on "cattle sick" country treated with White Island manure can be really proved. This alone, apart from actual manurial value, would be of untold value to a huge area of country should it prove to really cure or even mitigate this serious trouble, especially when the source of supply is so close to a great part of the country so troubled. In this connection we think trials of not only the present manure produced should be made, but also of the oxide product of the island, alone and in conjunction with the present manure.

"We also consider trials should be made of these White Island products in conjunction with other manures containing good percentages of phosphate of lime, such as superphosphate, ground Nauru phosphate rock and basic slag. . . .

"From this report you will gather that we realise that these products are something new in the way of manures and no one can yet judge fully whether the properties of these products are of actual manurial value or have the power of making available manurial values already in the soil either naturally or by previous application of manures. This must be found by experiment and is well worthy of being properly and fairly carried out."

While these events were in progress the shares were offered to the public. A newcomer, apparently of French origin, appeared on the scene. Since the rather florid name he gave at the time may well have been an alias, he can be called Dubois. He evidently made it his business to strike up an acquaintance with Miles, not only expressing great interest in the project, but also offering his help in selling the shares. He undoubtedly had a persuasive tongue, and at a meeting with Buttle it was agreed that he should receive a commission of 4% on any shares he was able to place. As he knew few likely prospects, he was given letters of introduction to brokers in various towns as far south as Christchurch, who in turn made available to him lists of their clients who might be interested. In the case of any sales made to these people he would be acting as a "half commission man," that is, he would be expected to share his earnings with the firms who put him in touch with the investors.

Dubois was, it seemed, short of money, for he borrowed £20 from Miles and, to help him on his way, collected a further £50 from G.A. Buttle & Co. as an advance against the sales he so confidently forecast. Nor was his optimism misplaced, since demands by telegram for additional sums of £50 to be sent to him on account of commission on substantial sales reached Auckland from widely scattered points.

Unfortunately these were not the only missives to arrive on Buttle's desk. It seemed that Dubois, with Gallic panache, evidently thought even the rosy view of the company's future

outlined in the prospectus did not do it full justice, and so proceeded to add further colour of his own. Wellingtonians, for
instance, were assured that an important merchant house
intended to take up shares in White Island Products and to
distribute its fertiliser, abandoning its existing valuable fran-
chise for a well-known brand of superphosphate in order to do
so. This claim seemed on the face of it so unlikely as to arouse
immediate suspicion.

In similar vein a farmer at Masterton was told that the
vendor, White Island Agricultural Chemical Co., had paid a
dividend of 30% the previous year, whereas in fact there was
none. This statement resulted in an exchange of telegrams
with Nicholson, whose reaction to even a suggestion of his name
being associated in any way with share-pushing activities may
well be imagined.

When Dubois returned to Auckland at the end of September
Buttle questioned him closely about his sales tactics, but he was
not giving anything away:

> "His obvious surprise and whole bearing in answering the
> charge suggests that there has been a mistake somewhere."

Confronted by a complete denial of all the allegations coming
from the south, there seemed to be only one thing to do. Miles,
an apparently sincere person and bearing the authority of a
director, left in October on a tour of much of the ground that
Dubois had covered, and was able to reassure many fears and
assuage ruffled feelings.

Dubois also claimed to have settled his dues to the brokers
who had put him in touch with their clients, but for months
afterwards claims came in for part commission which he had
not paid. In these circumstances it is little wonder that the
Frenchman thought it prudent to seek new fields for his energies.
He disappeared from Auckland "leaving quite a few lamenting
his departure," as Buttle put it. He himself had good reason
to be one of these for, while under no obligation to do so, his
firm settled the other brokers' accounts at a cost of £90. Miles's
loan of £20 was also never seen again.

At the end of the year the New Zealand Co-operative Dairy Co. decided not to give its support to White Island Products, but promoted instead a company to distribute superphosphate. This decision was quite reasonable, since the investigating committee had pointed out that the effectiveness of the White Island fertiliser was still largely an unknown quantity, and advocated trials lasting for at least three years to decide the matter. On the other hand, nobody had any doubts about superphosphate, and an extension of its use in the Waikato area must bring a much quicker increase in milk production since there would be no time lost in waiting for the results of field tests.

The action was, however, a serious blow to White Island Products. Not only had it lost the substantial capital and sales outlet which it had hoped to gain, but since this prospect had been given publicity its failure was no advertisement for the fertiliser. The newcomer to the trade, with such powerful backing, also inevitably brought price-cutting as each of the competing companies strove to retain its former share of the market.

Lower profit margins soon showed up the weakness of the White Island position. The quarried rock was ground in roller type mills, whose output would be far lower than that of the rotating drum ball mills which would probably be used today. It seems unlikely that production ever approached the figure forecast in August, 1926 of "at least 3,000 tons a month." The exposed situation of the island involved expensive delays in loading and transport; Mercer gave an instance of a by no means unusual incident:

> "I left the island at 3 o'clock yesterday afternoon, and after an hour or os we ran into a very heavy northerly gale, which blew us 14 miles out of the course, and forced us to creep up the coast, finally getting into Tauranga at 6 o'clock this morning."

When a 56 mile passage took fifteen hours it did nothing to help costs which were already too high.

Long and rough passages were not the worst of the transport

problem. At one time when *Paroto* was lying in Crater Bay, her anchor chain parted. She grounded broadside on to the boulder beach, having to be shored up until salvage could be attempted. Although she was generally referred to as a scow, my friend Clifford W. Hawkins, the well-known authority and writer on coastal shipping, maintains that this description was not correct. He knew her well, and told me she was really a normal round bottomed vessel, essentially power driven though also carrying sail to steady her in heavy weather.

The s.s. *Apanui* (Captain Keatly) was despatched from the Waitemata with suitable gear, including a large pump lent for the occasion by the Auckland Launch and Towboat Co. Mr R.J. Maney was on board to take part in the work of repairing and refloating the craft, and gave me an account of operations.

Since *Paroto* was on the beach it might be thought that repairs at any rate would be comparatively easy, but there were difficulties. The port bilge had been holed in three places by large boulders when she struck. It was impossible to patch the outside of the bottom of the hull as the ship was aground, so coffer dams had to be built round the holes.

These kept the ship as watertight as possible, and allowed the pump to make inroads on the internal flooding. When the bilges were reasonably clear the holes were sealed with concrete, and where it was possible to reach the outer surface additional patching with canvas and metal was applied.

The work went on for a week or so, and in his leisure moments Maney tried the fishing in Crater Bay. He was surprised to find that, despite the outflow from the acid stream, he was able to catch some quite sizeable snapper.

At last everything was ready for the refloating attempt. The islanders were naturally on hand to enjoy the free show. A towrope was secured between the two ships, but as the steamer took the strain Captain Rhyder of *Paroto* realised that the wire, passing round the stem, would cause damage as it was then rigged. A halt was called for anti-chafing gear to be put in place.

At a signal *Apanui* went ahead, and the jerk of the wire

coming taut caused a slight movement of the grounded vessel. Repetitions of this manoeuvre gradually brought her head round until it faced out to sea, but the stern was held fast by a propeller jammed ashore. This, however, gave up the unequal struggle when a blade snapped off, and *Paroto* was once again afloat after being stranded for a couple of weeks. The final bill for repairs ran into several thousand pounds.

The Northern Steam Ship Company's charge for shipping fertiliser worked out at about ten shillings a ton, including demurrage. This was certainly not unreasonable, since apart from the inevitable delays due to weather, the proposed bulk facilities for loading and discharge were never installed, so the wearisome manhandling of sacks continued to waste a lot of time. The important point was that this one item alone represented nearly 12% of the product's selling price of £4. 5s.0d. per ton on the rail at Tauranga.

The issue of capital proved to be a disappointment, for only about 26,000 of the 50,000 shares offered in New Zealand attracted subscribers. It was quite obvious that deep drilling would be necessary to establish the reserves of sulphur-bearing ore, also to construct and bring into production the appropriate refining plant would take both time and money. Since available funds were so much less than had been hoped, efforts were concentrated on the fertiliser to consolidate the company as a profitable concern. Work on sulphur was to be deferred until adequate finance was available, but as the price of the manure was no longer competitive because of price-cutting, the company was obliged to curtail output. As an alternative, drilling was started on the crater flat with a view to advancing the start of sulphur production.

Miles was sent off to Sydney to see if something on the lines of the abortive dairy company deal could be negotiated with an Australian distributor. At first things went well:

"I ran into a General Lloyd, a man I used to soldier with in India. He is being awfully kind, and doing everything he can to help me.

Quarrying ore at the foot of Troup Head

Tramway dump trucks about to enter the factory

Bagging fertiliser at the hoppers

Paroto moored at the jetty

"The business is progressing well, but it takes time, you can't rush it."

His efforts bore fruit, only to meet with a totally unexpected setback:

"I am rather out of touch here, and don't know exactly what is happening. You probably know that I had an offer from a good firm here to take 10,000 shares contingent on the company giving them the Australian agency, but the directors do not seem to see their way clear to do this. Their letter, in the post, will no doubt explain, but in the meantime I am very much at sea.

"My immediate problem is one of bread and butter, so I am not exactly working under the best conditions; in fact I am worried to hell. . . ."

As far as White Island Products was concerned, the arrangement was for directors to be paid a fee of £100 per annum, plus any additional remuneration which might be voted at a general meeting. Since the first annual meeting of members would not take place until the end of 1927, Miles was, apart from any private means he may have had, dependent upon advances by G.A. Buttle & Co. pending settlement of brokerage on the capital issue, which he was to share. His director's fee of less than £2 a week would not go far when living, as he was, first at the Union Club and later at the Imperial Service Club. He wrote,

"Sydney is a most expensive place, and though I am endeavouring to do things as cheaply as possible, some things one must do."

The company was, of course, liable to reimburse him for his out of pocket expenses while acting on its behalf, but it was proving far from prompt in meeting its obligations, both in this and other directions.

One cannot help feeling rather sorry for Miles, who appears to have been a basically honest man, trying to cope with a situation quite beyond him. It is to be hoped that, as seems to have been the case, when the opportunity came for him to dispose of his investment derived from the Canadian company he had the good sense to take advantage of it.

The reason for the rejection of the Australian offer lay in the activities of Mercer. Whilst his colleague was busy in Sydney, Mercer travelled further afield in search of additional finance. In January, accompanied by his family, he arrived in Vancouver. They at once fell victims to the prevailing influenza epidemic, but on his recovery Mercer discussed the liquidation of White Island Agricultural Chemical Co. with his legal friend Coburn, who was to undertake the task.

He also tried to arrange the sale of a controlling interest in White Island Products to an unnamed large American concern. He was, however, doubtful whether such a takeover would be allowed by the New Zealand Government, ever sensitive to foreign buying of local interests. Nothing came of the proposition, so he went on to London.

Mercer contacted the slumbering White Island (NZ) Sulphur and Fertiliser Co., which was to be renamed the White Island (New Zealand) Sulphur, Fertiliser and Development Co. Ltd. on 10 November. It no longer used Thame & Co.'s address, having taken an office of its own at Waterloo Place, S.W.1.

Despite the lukewarm reception of the share issue in New Zealand, the English company agreed to take up 40,000 immediately, with an option until 31 December 1929 to acquire at par all of the remaining 64,838 still available for subscription. Probably it was felt that another couple of years would disclose the viability or otherwise of the venture.

It is not clear why the Australian offer was turned down. Only 10,000 shares were involved, and it would seem that a possibly large outlet for the fertiliser would have been a great help to the company in view of the difficult situation on the New Zealand market.

With the prospect of new money becoming available, Kennedy, the resident engineer, pushed ahead with drilling. The tools he had to work with were far from satisfactory. The rig itself seems to have been a makeshift affair, largely of timber construction, which was too light for the task. It even blew over in a gale on 8 October. Many buried boulders were encountered during boring operations, and the apparatus frequently refused to pierce these, glancing off the hard and often slippery surface so that the bore was deflected and sometimes had to be abandoned.

The lightness of the rig had something to do with this, but Thame and Co., a London firm of mining consultants who acted as advisers, also condemned the type of bit in use as quite unsuitable. On one occasion when this was lost, and fishing failed to retrieve it, Gilberd had to go to Auckland for a replacement.

If sulphur was found, there was considerable difficulty in obtaining sufficient steam from either natural sources or the portable boiler to keep it molten. It often set like concrete, clogging pipes and other equipment. On occasion there was nothing for it but to lower a charge of gelignite down a bore to cut the piping, so that this could be withdrawn for use elsewhere.

In the event of a bore proving to be productive, a valve was fitted to the head of the casing so that it might be closed. If there was enough steam present, it could then build up pressure in the pipe to keep the ore in liquid condition.

Seawater was pumped to the drilling site, being used to lubricate the bit, cool down bores where natural steam was troublesome, also to flush out sand and stones. This supply experienced a variety of interruptions. Sometimes in rough weather the intake would be out of the sea periodically as the waves surged to and fro, while on other occasions it suffered blockage by sand, shingle, seaweed or even jellyfish.

Drilling did not follow a numerical sequence, bores being identified in accordance with a grid pattern for the crater flat, so that the first to be sunk was No. 108. The pleasing illusion of the whole crater being underlaid by molten sulphur was soon dispelled. As the weeks went by with no more than traces being found, Kennedy no doubt wondered if his luck would ever change.

It did so on 8 August, when the drilling rods suddenly slipped down at 85 feet in bore No. 123 and then stuck fast. He rightly deduced that the bit had dropped into sulphur which then solidified on cooling below 237°F. It was decided to close down for the night, hoping the heat below would build up again and release the equipment.

In the morning the rods were free. These were removed and replaced by a deep well pump in an effort to raise the now liquid material. Kennedy soon found that locating sulphur was only half the battle, for long before it reached the surface the pump stopped after working for only three minutes. This and the piping were lifted clear of the bore. Everything was immovably clogged, there being nothing for it but to spend the rest of the day on cleaning with the help of a blowlamp and fires lit under the pipe. Additional steam was later drawn from another bore, and sulphur was recovered for about a week.

A report was sent to Thame and Co. in London, and while awaiting their advice drilling continued at other locations, but with little success. In one case it took as much as eight hours to drill one foot through a boulder. Blowouts of steam, water and mud were common, and very low tides caused failure of the seawater supply because the intake was no longer submerged.

By 8 November instructions arrived from England, and Kennedy described the events which followed in a letter to Miles:

> "Recommendations to the head office to sink another bore about a chain and a half from 123 were acted upon, the bore being officially known as 122A. The best showing we had yet struck was evidenced here, liquid sulphur running into the hole at 100 feet, as it had done in No. 123.
>
> "We continued for a few yards to give the sulphur a good bottom (sandstone) to lie on, and then tried a home-made boiler — a length of pipe with a valve at the bottom — to see if we could exhaust the sulphur. However, the hole had evidently developed a big pressure at the bottom, and imme-

diately we drew the boiler we pulled the trigger, as it were, by releasing the pressure.

"Up she came, carrying a very fair quantity of sulphur in the steam jet — a gusher! Of course we were not prepared for this and all hands worked at the double getting the plant out of the way. In ten minutes there must have been several hundredweight of solid sulphur lodged all over the drum and gears of the plant. It was bubbling out in big spongelike semi-molten chunks — a glorious sight after our many disappointments.

"Most of it, however, was being blown by the steam jet into the air where it formed into a very fine dust almost blinding us when we were working round the plant. The sulphur setting round the mouth of the casing then commenced to block up the vent, and we had to knock the blobs off and hammer the casing with sledges to keep it clear.

"In this manner the pipe was kept open for two hours, after which we allowed it to become dormant. I should say that three or four tons of sulphur came up in that time, and that about a ton an hour was being ejected when we let her stop. . . .

"My theory as to the cause is that, in continuing to bore into the sandstone, we tapped a high pressure of steam which is coming up at such a terrific pace that it picks the sulphur up from a higher sulphur-bearing stratum and carries it to the surface, a natural high pressure steam lift. . . .

"My goodness, sir, the rum jar had a nasty jolt the night the gusher occurred!"

It became evident that a steam jacket round the bore would be essential to keep the sulphur molten, for during the next few days the pipe became completely choked. Special fittings for the casing head were ordered, and when these arrived efforts were made to lead steam from two nearby wells. In both instances however, the pipes split below ground, being too corroded to resist the steam pressure.

Kennedy therefore started a new bore, No. 160, with the

intention of using it both for prospecting and to provide the required steam supply. This was temperamental while drilling was in progress, and more excitement was in store:

"On arrival at No. 160 this morning (15 December) it was found that cracks had appeared round the hole and steam was issuing from them. When preparing to shift the plant, an upheaval of the ground surrounding the bore for a radius of about 20 feet occurred.

The ground rose about a foot, and on subsiding caused numerous large fissures through which steam commenced blowing. The plant was shifted immediately and subsequently steam and boiling water commenced to come up round the casing, developing into a furiously boiling hole with the casing suspended by the lead-off pipe in the centre."

Perhaps it was just as well that the staff was able to leave shortly afterwards to enjoy some relaxation during the summer vacation.

The volume of fertiliser output at Tauranga was not up to expectations, and instead of installing facilities for bulk loading and discharge of cargoes, as had been envisaged in the prospectus, it was decided to concentrate all production activities at the island, using Sulphur Point as the mainland store for distribution.

This entailed a major building programme on White Island, the site chosen being close to the quarry at the foot of Troup Head, despite the fact that on rare occasions in severe weather the sea had entered the crater flat at Wilson Bay and swept across this area to escape again at Crater Bay. No such flooding occurred during the time Gilberd was on the island. He and his friends successfully tackled the job of erecting the new factory in ferro-concrete, though not without some misgivings as to the possible effects of the acid fumes on their work.

An aspect of management arose which had possibly not been foreseen by some members of the board in Auckland. To go to White Island, or even Tauranga, in those days of poor land communications and no air service was a time-consuming affair.

Most of the local directors had their own businesses to look after in the city, so the actual operations of the company devolved very largely upon Mercer, who established his headquarters at the Dominion Building in Tauranga. He commuted between the port and White Island either by the company's launch *Whakaari* or the *Paroto*, which provided the main transport for the enterprise. Mr Walsh, who had formerly been in charge of sales, was promoted to assist him.

Mercer no doubt thought this state of affairs quite logical, since he not only had far more experience than anybody else in working the quarry and factory, but could also claim to be acting on behalf of both the Canadian and English interests. His colleagues in Auckland, however, had the uncomfortable feeling that they were little more than onlookers in the venture. Although the position was undesirable in view of their responsibility to the shareholders in New Zealand, it could be accepted if the undertaking was successful.

On 9 May 1928 the English company was rechristened a second time to become the New Zealand Sulphur Co. Ltd., having an authorised capital of £280,000 in £1 7½% cumulative preference shares participating up to 10%, and £35,000 in ordinary shares of one shilling each.

None of the 1923 directors still held office. Mercer was on the board in the company of Sir Park Goff, KC, MP, as chairman, Sir William Alexander, KBE, CB, CMG, DSO, MP, and John Goodenay (or Goodenday). George H. Duncan was the secretary.

These moves were connected with the liquidation of White Island Agricultural Chemical Co. In November 1926 the bondholders had received shares in White Island Products, including a bonus, in exchange for their interests. In addition Mercer, Miles, Clark and Schneeloch deposited a proportion of their own shares in a pool as a safeguard to the smaller holders.

All concerned now came to an agreement that if the New Zealand Sulphur Co. made a bid for all shares held in North America, the large shareholders would be released from the pool agreement. An offer was therefore made by the London company on 11 October 1928 by which:

    (a) Each White Island Products share could be exchanged for one New Zealand Sulphur Co. £1 preference share and one 1/– ordinary share, or

    (b) Sixteen shillings would be paid in cash for each White Island Products share.

As a result the New Zealand Sulphur Co. acquired about a further 84,000 shares.

It appears that many holders were astute enough to prefer the cash option, though Coburn and some of his friends elected to retain their interests in White Island Products. They possibly reasoned that if the London management, with all the facts before it, was prepared to take up a controlling interest, they could hardly lose by participating directly in a good thing.

The New Zealand Sulphur Co. never took up the option to subscribe for the remaining 64,838 unissued shares. Thus, although White Island Products became its subsidiary, the New Zealand company received no additional capital.

It could certainly have used this money, since there never seemed to be enough to undertake development with really adequate equipment on a large scale. Mercer was now accredited as the local representative of the London company, and his hold on affairs was therefore considerably strengthened. He notably increased output during 1929, when 2,930 tons of sulphur were shipped as compared with 900 in 1927 and 719 in 1928. Fertiliser production was also raised, and this was the busiest year the island had yet known.

In any mining venture costing can present problems, for it may be very difficult to draw a satisfactory line between expenses which may properly be capitalised as development work for amortisation against later production, and costs which should be charged against current profits. It was, for instance, believed early in 1929 that fertiliser was being sold profitably, but later in the year this was found to be wrong. It was therefore decided, in compliance with the wishes of the parent company, to concentrate all efforts for the present on working sulphur.

Company policy and the traditional see-saw certainly had something in common.

For some months Mercer was quite certain economic production of sulphur would become firmly established, but in July, 1930 his assistant Walsh advised the directors in Auckland of delays in the retorting process, which was prone to blockage by sand, and, contrary to the optimism of earlier reports, that ore reserves were now proving insufficient. He resigned shortly afterwards. Mercer was then on six months' leave.

These events brought yet another swing of the pendulum. The New Zealand Sulphur Co. sent out an engineer from England, David Gilmour, to reorganise the fertiliser side of the business. Reliance was still placed on the No. 1 Product, consisting mainly of material drawn from the Troup Head quarry. The sulphur content was generally far below the figure of "nearly 50%" mentioned in the prospectus, and as the specification stipulated a level of 40% in the manure, this had to be attained by additions of high quality sulphur stripped from the fumaroles.

Like its predecessor, the company firmly believed in the efficacy of the mineral as a manure, and collected further evidence in support of this view from various official sources such as the British Ministry of Agriculture and research institutes in the United States. Among the latter were the Pullman Agricultural Station, Washington, the Coastal Plains Experimental Station in Georgia and the University of Missouri.

The central point of all these researches was the increased yield of legumes, roots and various other crops resulting from the application of sulphur, also the rate at which it was removed from the soil by the demands of plant life. Figures produced by the institutes and others revealed that in the case of some crops the yields were doubled by intensive feeding with sulphur, also certain vegetables, such as cabbages and turnips, might absorb as much as 100 lbs. per acre.

There was always the snag, of course, that while No. 1 Product had the sulphur content as its main selling theme, it still lacked the equally important phosphate of lime. This was the objection raised by the investigating committee appointed by the New Zealand Co-operative Dairy Co. In an attempt to meet it, a mixture was evolved which incorporated 16% of Nauru Island phosphate with 84% of No. 1 Product, but this was not sold on any considerable scale.

It had been hoped that the guano beds at the gannet colonies would provide a valuable ancillary source of fertiliser, since the thousands of birds lived on an exclusive diet of fish, the manurial qualities of which are well-known. This possibility was encouraged by the example of the islands off the coast of Peru populated by immense numbers of cormorants, known as guanos. There was, however, one important difference. The western seaboard of South America in that latitude is famous for having one of the driest climates in the world. Whatever other natural resources White Island may lack, rainfall is definitely not one of these. It was therefore found that much of the soil nutrient had been leached out of the guano. It was mixed experimentally with No. 1 Product, but was not found to be a commercial proposition. However deep the deposits may have been, these were left almost entirely undisturbed. The birds were able to continue to make their annual visits to breed, and were treated affectionately as pets by the island staff.

The accounts presented to the shareholders at the fourth annual general meeting in December, 1930 made gloomy reading. The loss for the year was put at £7,815, making the total to date £27,466. In addition to this, over-valuations and brokerage stood on the assets side of the balance sheet at £10,478, no profits having yet been earned which would have permitted these items to be written off. Land, buildings and plant were shown as being worth £138,554. Whilst this probably represented actual cost, possibly less some depreciation, such a valuation could only be sustained whilst the business was a going concern. The £42,000 profit taken by the White Island Agricultural Chemical Co. represented an over-capitalisation which lay as a deadweight on its struggling successor.

Trading conditions generally did nothing to help the company in its difficulties, for the Wall Street crash of 1929 had sparked off the great world depression, which hit New Zealand hard. One farmer told me he had to sell butterfat for sixpence a pound at the time. As might be expected in such circumstances, bad and doubtful debts from fertiliser sales figured in the accounts.

It was perhaps symptomatic that after the post office on the island closed down on 22 December, when the company's staff left for their Christmas holidays, it did not reopen on their return. It had at least achieved the distinction of providing latter-day philatelists with one of the rarest cancellations in New Zealand postal history.

While on the subject of Christmas, Buttle met men who worked on the island for as long as eight years, going to the mainland only for their annual leave. It was an odd, monastic sort of life, but they do not appear to have been unduly troubled by seeing no women, other than the occasional visitor, from one year's end to the next.

On one occasion a film company provided both feminine attractions and visitors in plenty. The venture lasted for about three days, and a flotilla of launches brought the large party, including about sixty Maoris as "extras" from Whakatane. While the local talent chose a warm area on the ground to sleep, so that no form of covering was necessary, the camp supply of blankets was still taxed to its utmost to provide them with costumes.

Acting was not without its difficulties. For one scene the Maoris were required to run down a slope. This was covered with small stones, none too comfortable for bare feet normally used to the protection of footwear. Their consequent lack of dash was the cause of some exacerbation between themselves and the director.

The latter also had a problem with an actor who was scheduled to spring from below the ground, simulating terror of the nether regions. Even in this setting he evidently had trouble in making his fears seem sufficiently convincing. At last, hot and weary from repeated attempts to please his taskmaster, he sank down on a rock to rest, but accidentally put one hand on a small jet of superheated steam. There was certainly nothing faked about his performance then, even though it may not have been quite what the director had in mind.

The romantic interest was supplied by an actress who was a determined feminist. When confronted by the admittedly difficult terrain she was heard to declaim loudly:

"Where an American man can go, an American woman can go too!"

The destination was the camp, first entailing the climb out of the crater by what was known as the staircase. This was the section of the track which mounted in a serpentine fashion up the very steep slope of the crater wall, the scene of occasional accidents. With some encouragement from the onlookers she climbed over the rim, but when she reached the flimsy-looking bridges spanning ravines her nerve failed her, and she had recourse to despised male assistance to cross. Evidently this was one occasion when her conviction would have been better left unsaid.

Generally speaking, the island had little to offer in the way of recreation. For those with a fondness for the bottle, freedom from tiresome enforcement of the licensing laws was at least a distinct point in its favour. The few beaches were strewn with large boulders, and bathing was not particularly safe. The loose surface, steep slopes and numerous gullies did little to encourage those who felt like taking a stroll anywhere except on the works track. I have been told that on occasion the men were known (though not in Gilberd's time) to go as far as Opotiki for cinema visits, but it would surely seem the film would need to be very good if it was to justify a round trip of about sixty miles.

The fishing, however, was first-class, one of the best grounds being near and even between the towering Volkner Rocks, though in some places long lines were needed to reach the bottom. There are photographs in existence showing hapuka of virtually big game fish proportions hoisted on the camp derrick. Crayfish and octopus could be taken alnog the shore not far from the camp, and with supplies straight from the sea the cook was able to prepare fish courses of a quality which lived long in the memories of the staff. Line fishing sometimes gave place to the quicker method of explosives.

The isolation of the place helped to keep the staff free from the usual run of infection. The fumes from the volcano did not adversely affect their health, and even seemed to be beneficial in some cases. Gilberd was cured of asthma during those years, though his hearing was affected. The innocuous results of exposure to the fumes was really a rather surprising feature, for there was no doubt about their potency. Buttle wrote:

> "I was once called on by a man who wanted to buy a long boat that he said he had found with the new cut timber all shaped and holed ready to be put together. It was, of course, the old boat used to take the men from the camp to the crater flats. All bolts, copper nails and paint had dissolved, leaving the planks like new."

By March, 1931 he had become a director, to help the company in what he termed, with good reason, "its rocky progress." By then his colleague Macmillan was looking after affairs at Tauranga pending Gilmour's return from overseas. Mercer, then in London, had been absent from New Zealand for so long that under the articles of association he had forfeited his directorship. Nicholson had now lost confidence in the company, and Rogerson took over his seat on the board. The two believed White Island Products to be a lost cause which might well have to be wound up, though this was rather prejudging events.

By this time the enterprise had reached its fullest state of development. The camp had become quite a comfortable place, with electric lighting. A billiard room with an adjoining library was provided for recreation in the evenings. A two roomed guest house with a verandah, sited close to the Ohauora "a" gannet colony at the camp landing place, accommodated casual visitors staying overnight.

In one instance it was used for five and a half weeks during the school holidays by Gilberd's wife and three children, the latter probably being the first youngsters to stay on the island. For the first fortnight, when the engineer looked after things while the rest of the staff was away for Christmas, the family had the whole island to themselves. Gilberd reported daily by radio to the company's office at Tauranga, while Mrs Gilberd fended off searching questions from her anxious children as to how Santa Claus would get there.

The provision of an adequate water supply was always a problem. The island itself, by its very nature, was singularly ill-equipped to be of much use in this respect for several reasons. The catchment area was rather limited. The steepness of the slopes caused a very rapid run-off. There were no permanent streams, and the only pond was an artificial one created by a concrete dam built by the Canadian company, surely with extreme difficulty, across a large gully at a point high up on the very steep outer face of the cone near Crater Bay. This was intended to supply feed water for the works boilers, but seems to have received little use.

Although the loose and porous terrain was often of little value for collecting underground supplies, a well sunk at the camp to a depth of twenty-eight feet provided hot water for baths and washing clothes until a large cistern was installed to collect rainwater. When heavy demands were made upon supplies from the well, the temperature rose to an uncomfortable extent, and had to be cooled down from a surface tank.

Drinking water was brought from Tauranga in tanks and petrol cans, the latter not always too well cleaned of their former contents. This was supplemented by a plant capable of distilling sixty gallons of seawater a day. Gilberd recalled:

> "It was very crude, and the fire smoked so badly that the clean water dropping out of the end of the condenser used to get well smoked."

There was also a smaller but more efficient still for drinking purposes at the factory.

The cook was obviously a key figure in sustaining morale in this isolated situation, and food supplies needed careful or-

ganisation when the island could be cut off from the mainland
for as long as three weeks at a time:

"Meat used to come in quite big lots, and the butcher
would put it aboard on Sunday evening so that it was fresh
when we got it on Monday morning. It just used to come in a
sack up to 2 cwt. at a time. The cook had six or eight 4 gallon
tins of dripping, and meat that had to be kept was half-
cooked and then dumped into tins of molten fat. We would
then have fresh sausages for breakfast ten days after a boat
had been and a nice hot roast sirloin up to a fortnight, if
he knew in time to have ordered enough to last that long.

"Fish was a great help but we could not get that if the
weather was very bad. We once did a bit of a starve when
two tins of meat came instead of the two cases ordered. We
did eat 'Solan Goose' (gannet) then after four days on fish.
We had very few hens at that time, though for a while we
had about forty.

"In October we used to gather muttonbird eggs. They
were mostly used for making cakes, but were quite good boiled
or fried. The white was harder than in duck eggs. These
were not eggs laid in nests but ones they just dropped anywhere. After one stormy night the cook gathered over 100,
and often over 60 without taking one that would have
hatched.

"The cook was a wonderful breadmaker, and his cakes,
etc., were very good too. Meat, vegetables, puddings and
stews were very, very good and his soups were special. He
had one ordinary 'Orion' range and a large double-ovened
one, with Christmas tree wood firing, cut by circular saw.
The cook's helpers served the plates of food out usually,
though some of us used to walk through one end of the
kitchen and be given a plate as we passed through. We
helped ourselves to tea served in 4 gallon tins with taps."

Since in 1969 Gilberd was in his eighties and enjoying his
retirement, there could evidently have been little wrong with
this diet.

The same was also largely true for animals then on the island:

"Usually we had some sheep out there as a standby for fresh meat supply. They were on the north-west side of the island. Once about a dozen were sent over. They stayed round the camp and tried to eat some grass near the guest house, but it was too tough for them. Then evidently one tried a bush of taupata (Coprosma) near my hut, and next day they had eaten it down to stems about as big as my thumb.

In a few days they had eaten all the taupata round the camp and followed bushes along the western way, finally finding the one track near the crater rim where it was possible to pass a big lava flow and thus get over to the north-west, where there was plenty of taupata. A bit later we shot one, and it was rolling fat. They were all very fat, and this was all there was for them to eat."

There was also a terrier on the island for a time.

In a cleared area near the camp attempts were made to grow various fruits, including apples and grapes, but none thrived. Vegetables also were spoiled by rain when the wind was blowing from the north-east. It then collected fumes as it fell, reaching the plants in the form of dilute acid. For this reason too the guttering on the huts was made of wood.

Since there was no motor transport outside the crater, the most convenient way of collecting supplies of fuel for the camp was by gravity. A "flying fox" was rigged from a point high in the forest, so that after a tree had been felled and cut up into convenient lengths the firewood travelled rapidly and effortlessly down to the living quarters.

The company may no longer have owned the launch which Mercer had described as a "magnificent seaboat", and used for travelling to and from the island. On one fateful occasion it carried a fishing party to Mayor Island, and broke a connecting rod in the engine. Although the mechanic managed to get the *Whakaari* safely back to port its ferrying days were over. There remained four craft, two of which were former lifeboats each

A load of fertiliser is hauled out to *Paroto*. Club Rocks lie beyond the empty pontoon

An open air laboratory test of a sample at the camp on the southern benches

Fresh crayfish f
dinner. A haul at Bu
galow Beach

Ohauora "c" ganne
colony. Club Rock
are seen at the left

thirty-six feet long, used for travelling between the camp and Crater Bay, also for fishing expeditions. Two sturdy pontoons plied from the concrete breakwater cum jetty to scows lying offshore, taking out fertiliser and sulphur in exchange for incoming items such as steam coal and machinery.

Ashore, the tramway linking the quarry at Troup Head, the factory building and Crater Bay was still in operation, with half a dozen three-quarter-yard tip trucks as its rolling stock. The line now entered the raw material store at the northern end of the works by means of a ramp, and the track was laid across the stringers of the roof. The wagons were hauled up the incline by means of a stationary engine, and discharged their loads inside the building for processing.

No doubt on the grounds of both economy in construction of access and flexibility of operation, motor transport was considered more suitable than a tramway to serve the scattered sulphur deposits. One road connected Wilson and Crater Bays. Another skirted the northern edge of the hummocks left by the lahar, and ended at the foot of Crater Ridge, the plateau which had been formed at the western end of the flat by the landslip of 1914. A Fordson tractor, fitted with a front end loader, and two of the famous Model T Ford trucks moved supplies of sulphur ore to the works. The acid fumes were hard on any form of metal plant, and the working life of the vehicles was fairly short. One engineer stated that if a lorry was used on the island for six months it would then be worth not more than a third of its original cost. In another case the manager told Gilberd to instal a metal pipe to collect gas samples from a fumarole. Within a short time all that remained of it was a corroded stump projecting from the socket.

The new works building was a far cry from its small wooden predecessor. Sited in line with the tramway, it extended along much of the track, being 250 feet in length by 52 feet wide, including a range of rooms in a lean-to attached to the main structure. The walls and floor were solidly built in ferro-concrete, while the roof of Oregon pine was sheathed with corrugated asbestos.

97

Part of the original fertiliser raw material store, 100 feet long, was appropriated to house the sulphur refining plant. This consisted principally of 5 six ton capacity brick lined retorts, with a smaller experimental one of 30 cwts., mounted in the form of a raised battery along one wall. These vessels varied considerably in working steam pressures from 30 to 70 lbs. A stationary main boiler supplied these, also the heating needed to dry the fertiliser.

It is perhaps rather surprising that this burned coal instead of oil. The work of loading and discharging solid fuel for transport by scow was tedious, not to mention the added chore of clearing away the ash. The choice of this mode of firing seems out of keeping with Mercer's usually progressive ideas.

Upon its arrival from the quarry, the fertiliser rock was first broken down in the central grinding room by means of a 15 cwt. single roll pug mill, then ground to the required degree of fineness in two double roller mills. Drying and screening were carried out in a 60 feet rotary drier or kiln. The completed product was carried by a bucket type elevator into the third division of the factory, the bagging store. It was distributed by the conveyor into three 80 ton capacity concrete hoppers, on two sides at the foot of which were platforms where men filled and weighed the sacks, then stacked these for shipment.

The most important part of the lean-to area of the factory was the engine room. In addition to the steam-raising plant, it housed the 72 h.p. Tangye semi-diesel engine which supplied power for the machinery, all of which was operated by belt drive. There was a small electric generating unit for lighting only. A doorway led into the fitter's shop, but this was not equipped for anything much more complicated than pipe-fitting or smithing. A store for tools and supplies completed the engineering department.

The remaining room in the main building was the laboratory, which led off the grinding room. There was always quite a lot of assaying required to ensure that the 40% sulphur content of the fertiliser was maintained, also to determine the richness of the ore being won for refining. Apart from the factory was the housing of the winch for operating the big derrick at Crater Bay, also a small office. The latter was subsidiary to the main one, which was situated in the more salubrious area of the camp.

At Tauranga a new building had been erected in concrete, but the rather ramshackle old one was still retained to form an extension of the new structure. There was another small hut used as a laboratory and kitchen. The jetty was showing signs of its age and the heavy traffic which had passed over it, having attracted some criticism from the harbour master.

The position had deteriorated further since the end of the previous financial year in June, 1930 and it began to look as though the enterprise was beyond saving. Calls made upon partly-paid shares held by the London company were in arrear. Since the National Bank of New Zealand had allowed White Island Products to overdraw its account, it had a distinct interest in the settlement of these unpaid calls, and accepted an appointment as the company's agent in England to try to effect collection.

The need for funds was indeed desperate. As an economy measure two employees were dismissed. The company was liable to pay compensation for failing to fulfil its advertising contract. More important was the fact that the Northern Steam Ship Co. had suspended shipments from the island until its outstanding account for freight was paid. This service was obviously vital to the continued existence of the business, and a directors' meeting was adjourned whilst Mr W.T. Strand, the chairman, had a consultation with Captain Hammond. An agreement was reached whereby the shipping company would move a further 400 tons of fertiliser to Tauranga provided that the stock already at the port was pledged as security for payment.

Difficult though things undoubtedly were for White Island Products, the unhappy New Zealand Sulphur Co. in London was in an even worse plight. Since nearly all of its funds were invested in the operating company, it was obviously dependent for income upon dividends from that source. None had yet been forthcoming nor, it appeared, were ever likely to be unless its fortunes underwent a dramatic improvement.

The only other interest held by the New Zealand Sulphur Co. was described as "patent rights acquired from Thame." While no details are available, these were assumably connected with either the production or utilisation of sulphur, probably the former. These rights were in any case thought to be of doubtful value.

Like its subsidiary, the London company had issued only part of its capital. If the White Island venture fulfilled even a reasonable quota of the high hopes with which it had been launched, a fair measure of success would no doubt have enabled the parent company to find subscribers for the balance of its capital. But who would put money into an investment consisting predominantly of preference shares, the dividend on which was already years in arrear?

Nor was this all, for two of the directors, Alexander and Goodenay, claimed that they had been induced to take up their holdings by mis-statements in the prospectus. If this was anything like that of White Island Products, they were probably fully justified in their expressed intention of instituting legal proceedings against the company.

It was arranged to hold a general meeting of shareholders on 10 June, to be followed by a meeting of creditors. The first gathering, however, took on a note of farce, since all but one of the directors and also the secretary resigned *en bloc*. As if this was not enough, the company was in addition under notice to quit from its offices, so the sole remaining director was left with a homeless, semi-bankrupt business on his hands.

The creditors had little alternative but to postpone their meeting until such time as the situation resolved itself to some extent. The debts amounted to only about £4,000, most of which represented calls due to the subsidiary. These liabilities might, of course, be substantially increased if the actions by Alexander and Goodenay were successful, since their shareholdings were large ones.

Sulphur was in those days more subject to fluctuations of both

100

price and supply than it has been since large new sources became available. The New Zealand Sulphur Co. succeeded in convincing the Barter Trading Corporation Ltd., which formed part of the extensive Tennant financial interests in London, that it would be worth making a thorough investigation of the potential value of the remaining resources of White Island. The dissident shareholders were persuaded to defer taking any steps for the present which might make a successful revival of the enterprise an impossibility.

Whether Mercer had any hand in this new arrangement is not known, but it appears he no longer played any active part in affairs afterwards. His role in the attempted exploitation of the property had been both a long and important one. Although there may well have been times when he heartily wished he had never heard of the place, life during the two decades from 1913 was certainly never dull, and the drive he displayed could only have been equalled by his unquenchable optimism. One wonders how he came out of the affair financially; had he chosen a less hazardous and more rewarding avenue for his activities, he might easily have become a very wealthy man.

At this time White Island Products was in a moribund condition. The men were withdrawn from the island and dismissed, leaving behind them a large stock of fertiliser already bagged for sale and 20 tons of refined sulphur, as well as a further 250 tons of ore awaiting treatment. Nothing could be done without an injection of new capital. The long and unprecedentedly severe trade depression had destroyed business confidence, and the company's profitless record precluded any chance of raising more money locally.

Although as a subsidiary it was bound to carry out the orders of the New Zealand Sulphur Co., the latter recognised that the local directors felt a sense of obligation to creditors in New Zealand. It therefore decided to discharge these liabilities and appoint nominees to replace the elected directors. The funds for this and other needs were apparently supplied by the Barter Trading Corporation on the understanding that when the total amount of the advances was known this would be covered by a debenture. If the patent rights were in fact of no value, the only assets which could be pledged as security were evidently the freeholds of Sulphur Point and White Island, plus the plant and machinery.

A meeting was arranged in Auckland, which was attended by Buttle and Rogerson acting as directors representing the New Zealand creditors. The claims were met in full, whereupon the nominees of the parent company took office. When the business was concluded, Buttle said in jocular vein:

"Well, now you've got the island what are you going to do with it? If you want to sell, I'll give you £100."

Considering the sum which had just been paid, the new masters were not amused by this sally, but it is interesting as an indication of the direction in which Buttle's thoughts were turning even then. He always believed that the New Zealand Sulphur Co. had been taken over by Imperial Chemical Industries Ltd., but recent enquiries have proved this was not the case. It is, of course, possible the giant concern might have been interested as a customer for sulphur had it been available on a large scale.

Once again, as so often before, the future hinged upon the adequacy or otherwise of the sulphur ore reserves on the island. It was early in 1933 by the time the New Zealand Sulphur Co. commissioned Mr S.J.G. Goosman, an engineer with considerable experience of tin mining in Malaya and generally of high repute, to take a team to White Island to make a careful appraisal of the position.

Mr P.J. Hayman, who was acting as a nominee director, went to the island with Goosman for a preliminary survey on 17 March. On their return they engaged nine men to form the party, which was composed of:

Radio Operator, who was in charge of the camp
Mechanic
Assayer
Cook
Five labourers

The first two and three of the labourers had previously worked on the island, a fact of considerable importance to Goosman, since they were able to identify locations and their knowledge of conditions helped him with the preliminary work. The party embarked with the necessary stores, and arrived at White Island on 25 March.

The mountain did not take kindly to having its peace once more disturbed by human intruders, since at the end of the following week it staged a gala performance for their benefit. Although Goosman may not have thought so at the time, it is fortunate that a skilled observer was present to be able to record the event, also to give his appreciation of its effects in the crater.

On 2 April the peace of a summer Sunday morning was rudely shattered at 5.30 a.m. by a rumbling noise and a slight earthquake. This overture was trifling when compared with the eruption from the great blowhole known as Big Donald. As it got into its stride, half-ton boulders were tossed over 300 feet into the air. An ash shower spread over the island, the dust falling on the camp containing 4.7% of sulphur. Activity continued all day, shrouding White Island in a "cloud of steam, fumes and volcanic ash which extended far out to sea and shut out the sun." Luckily on the following day a strong wind cleared the air.

When Goosman was able to inspect the crater flat he found that a large, roughly circular area at the foot of the western plateau (also known as Crater Ridge) had collapsed. This was about 300 yards west of Big Donald, while both to the north and south of the blowhole the surface had also subsided, though only to little over a foot in depth. This led him to conclude that the new deep round depression, afterwards called the 1933 Crater, with the other sunken areas, were connected underground to Big Donald. He formed the theory that the material erupted had been supplied from the "cave-in" of the surrounding ground.

The men devoted six weeks to their task, making as careful examination as their means permitted. The drilling equipment could not be used as it was "scattered around in pieces." A

103

programme of deep drilling would probably have been outside their instructions, and Goosman contented himself with what results he could obtain from a modified posthole borer. This was supplemented by the use of a length of pipe, which was driven into the ground and kept constantly turning with a wrench so as to obtain a sample core.

At times this was difficult to secure, since ground temperatures in the crater were usually high, so that when loose ash, sand and scoria were withdrawn these dried rapidly and did not form the desired stratigraphic column from the intersected material in the normal way. On the other hand the ground could vary considerably in compactness, since close to Troup Head a conglomerate of boulders, pebbles and sand had set as hard as concrete.

The maximum depth reached by these rather crude methods was no more than six feet, though in some cases this was increased by the stratagem of boring from the bottom of a trench. Even this shallow boring was more than enough in certain sections of the flat, where rock or hot water were found only two or three feet below the surface, the latter often being a nuisance to prospecting. When I told Gilberd of this work he dismissed it as quite useless, since the minimum depth at which he found sulphur of any consequence was 65 feet, and his best strike was at 319 feet.

On locating a sulphur bed, Goosman would carry out trenching to determine its limits, also to provide information on the quantity of overburden which would have to be removed for mining. This was often a crucial matter, since if the amount was large its removal, perhaps mainly by hand labour, might be justified in the case of a rich seam, but could be uneconomic if the ore was only a medium or low grade.

There was, for example, a gypsum band examined on the coast "east of Wilson Bay" (assumably at the foot of the northern side of Troup Head):

"This averaged 7% sulphur but is beneath 31 feet of overburden. To attempt to mine even a medium grade ore as low priced as sulphur from under this class of overburden would be impossible."

Ore of 10% sulphur content was the minimum he had been asked to consider.

Goosman kept a sharp lookout for gypsum because it could indicate the presence of sulphur:

"In almost every case where a gypsum bed is found, the formation of sulphur is going on. As the larger seam. . . lies horizontally in one of these beds and, at several points, merges into gypsum between the same walls, the seam was evidently formed in this manner when, as has been proved, this section was a fumarole area emitting sulphuretted hydrogen and sulphur dioxide, as do all the gypsum beds beneath the fumaroles."

One interesting formation was unique among those he investigated.

"The extraordinary thing about the block of ore, of 40 tons of 36% in sight now at the end of the wharf, is that the track line, to lower the pontoons to the water, is only two feet above it. To delimit the small seams or block I sank three pits and bores behind it, to 18 feet, 11 feet and 9 feet, at a distance of 30 feet from the face with the first two and midway between the pit and waterfront with the third. Two of the pits went below water or sea level. I failed to find the ore and am convinced that it is a piece of a larger block that was washed from the old lake bed by the slide of 1914; it is probable that much sulphur was washed to sea at that time. The block is two feet thick and has the appearance of having solidified in a bed of small pebbles and fragments of rock, gravel and sand, such as would be found on the lake bottom."

The flat and other areas within the crater generally showed very low values of 4% or less, and where richer deposits were located these were sometimes beset by formidable working difficulties:

105

"I took a general sample from 6 points, to a depth of one foot, and obtained a result of 18.2% sulphur. The temperature at the surface is 85 degrees Fahrenheit and, at one foot, 140 degrees. While the men worked they took the precaution to stand on stones brought from a distance and I consider that the exploitation of this particular area would be difficult due to the temperature, situation and necessary expenditure to connect it with the lower flat."

The lay observer was also liable to be misled even by the evidence of his own eyes:

"The face of the cliff and, in fact, the whole interior of the crater area, appears to be sulphur from a distance. The colouring is iron pyrite, which the large blowhole frequently ejects, burnished by the fumes which never cease rolling up the cliffs."

The fumaroles were undoubtedly the source of really high grade deposits:

"I made a test, by placing a box over an active fumarole, leaving only a small opening for the escape of steam. In 100 hours the box collected a few ounces of crystal sulphur of 96.5%. The fumaroles were stripped during recent years, and the sulphur used in the fertiliser product. One could not collect half a ton from the whole crater. But the bases of these small vents are of rich sulphur and old fumarole areas have yielded a high grade."

Goosman was finally able to prepare his estimate of the sulphur then available. Stocks had been left at the works when operations ceased:

20 tons of retorted sulphur (96.5%)
440 tons sacked and in hoppers (28.7%)
700 tons in the retort room (11.5%)
5 tons in the dryer room (16.0%)
10 tons outside the factory (43.7%)

The 26 deposits he assessed as reserves economic for mining

in the crater totalled 3031.8 tons, likely to produce 560 tons of fine sulphur. In addition to these there was a bed near Troup Head known as the Pit, which could not be profitably worked because of the heavy overburden, also others on the western plateau and the northern slopes of the cone which would require heavy capital outlay to be brought into production. These almost certainly uneconomic areas could have contained sufficient ore to supply 387 tons of refined sulphur.

If further production was intended, it would be necessary to make a preliminary outlay which he put at £415 before it could commence. This included transport to the island, road building, repairs to buildings and the depreciation on a new motor truck. Mining by a staff of six men would cost £7.12.7d. a day, excluding a cook, whose wage would be recovered from catering charges paid by the miners. Working the deposits would take six months, and the ore could be placed at Crater Bay for 7s. 8d. per ton. He made no attempt to calculate the cost of refining, no doubt considering the quantity of ore available did not justify any further capital expenditure under this heading.

Goosman stated quite decisively "there is no tonnage of sulphur ore, for commercial purposes, available on White Island." Had his opinion of the quantity of reserves been favourable, the 20 tons of refined sulphur was to be sent to England for experimental purposes, but in view of his findings it was left at the works for disposal with the other assets.

It may be thought strange that Goosman made no mention of deep drilling in his report. There was, however, a complete set of records already available covering this work between 1927 and 1930. These showed the occurrence of sulphur at depth to have been sporadic, while production during the period from this source had proved to be quite uneconomic.

There would thus have been no point in going to the expense of putting down additional bores, since further mineral supplies were unlikely to have accumulated in any quantity since previous operations ceased. In the final stages before the company stopped work ore had been quarried, entailing the removal of large tonnages of overburden. This was no doubt the reason for Goosman's particular attention to the point.

After his very definite condemnation of the project there was a long pause for consideration of the position. Sulphur refining was, on the evidence, a lost cause. The most likely alternative might have been a fairly short-term venture based on fertiliser, the gypsum disclosed by the survey, and possibly the export of crude sulphur ore. There was only a slim chance that this would have been a paying proposition.

It was decided not to make any further attempt to work the property, and a debenture was executed in favour of the Barter Trading Corporation, in whose name Sir William Alexander, George F. Duncan and Annis Dora White applied for the appointment of a receiver or manager for the New Zealand Sulphur Co. in the same month. No doubt because the long-deferred actions against the company were now pending, the court did not immediately appoint a receiver.

The winding up of the parent company would involve the dissolution also of its subsidiary, whose assets had been pledged. An Auckland accountant, Mr W.J.A. Thomson, was appointed receiver for White Island Products on 20 September.

The cases against the London company were heard in the Chancery Division in the middle of September. Goodenay contended that he had been induced, by misrepresentation in the prospectus, and non-disclosure of material facts by certain persons on behalf of the company, to subscribe for 17,693 preference and 87,000 ordinary shares at a cost of £22,043. He applied for rescission of the contract and the removal of his name from the register of members. In a parallel action, David Kernan replaced Alexander. The sum involved here was £27,242, representing 22,500 preference and 94,844 ordinary shares.

The company denied the allegations, and pleaded that if any mis-statements had been made, these were issued without the defendant's authority, knowledge or consent. It further argued that the plaintiffs were debarred by delay and acquiescence from obtaining the relief they now claimed. Mr

Justice Crossman was not impressed by the defence. He found in favour of the plaintiffs, with costs, after a hearing which lasted 36 days.

Goodenay and Kernan could feel well satisfied with the verdict, but as things turned out they had won a Pyrrhic victory. The amount eventually realised from the sale of the assets was so low that the company was quite unable to comply with the terms of the judgments so far as restitution was concerned. The plaintiffs could not have foreseen this state of affairs, no doubt believing, reasonably enough, that the comparatively large sum appearing on the balance sheet in respect of land, buildings and plant in New Zealand had at least some basis in fact.

On 17 December Mr Justice Eve appointed William Gilbert Antrobus, CA, as receiver in the compulsory winding-up of the New Zealand Sulphur Co. The company did not finally disappear until it was dissolved under section 295 of the Companies Act by notice in the London Gazette on 27 January 1942.

In New Zealand Thomson dealt first with the property at Tauranga, which was comparatively easy to sell. The site is occupied today by a fish processing plant.

Tenders were called for the island assets in two lots, one for the freehold and the other for the machinery and stores. The sale of the island was a slow affair. At first Australian interests proposed to establish a plant to produce salt from the sea by evaporation, using the geothermal steam. Although at that time little was known of the use of natural steam as a source of heat and power, its value has been amply demonstrated in recent years in drying sawn timber at Kawerau and by the large electricity generating station at Wairakei.

Gilberd experimented by running seawater into lead trays and leaving it to evaporate, but the salt won tended to be discoloured. It is very questionable whether the natural limitations of the place would have permitted salt to be produced at a price competitive with the output from larger solar installations such as those in the South Island and near Adelaide.

The Sydney syndicate paid a deposit, but failed to pay the balance to complete the contract, so the property was put up for sale a second time. Buttle intended to put in a bid, but being detained in his office on the closing day he failed to do so. An irregularity was then found in the tender documents, so offers had to be called for a third time.

On this occasion Buttle took his completed form to Thomson just before tenders closed on the last day. As he handed it over he asked if the liquidator proposed to take time to consider the bids. The latter, probably rather tired of the whole troublesome business, replied:

"No, I will open these now. If you like to wait outside for five minutes I can let you know the answer."

Buttle did so, and shortly afterwards the accountant's head appeared round the door:

"The island is yours." .

This was confirmed on 22 June 1936.

V

Conservation Takes Over

The new owner commented that "he rather liked the idea of owning a volcano." The island's spell really went far deeper than this, for many years afterwards he wrote:

"I am setting myself the impossible task of trying to let you have some idea of the fascination that White Island has for us. . . . Strange as it may seem, the island is unbelievably beautiful and beyond description. Surely it is one of the wonders of the world. . . ."

He had a copy of Goosman's report, which contained a passage:

"There is a very large tonnage of gypsum on the north coast, but of what value it is I am unable to say. If it were worth exploiting, the ore could be transported to the coast by aerial ropeway very cheaply. The distance is not more than 250 yards with a fall from 500 feet. The gypsum is easily broken and would be rapidly and cheaply loaded into buckets."

Gypsum is a mineral always in demand in the manufacture of plaster of Paris and as a retarder in Portland cement. This deposit on the northern slopes contained sulphur varying between 24.6% and 45.1% purity, which was far better than the usual average. The seam had possibilities, and Buttle felt he would like to discuss it with Goosman, one point in particular which he wished to confirm being the "very large tonnage." Since Goosman's experience had been mainly in tin mining, his idea of a big quantity might be quite different from that accepted in, for instance, the coal industry.

The proposed meeting was by no means easy to arrange:

"After much difficulty and many months I got him into the office. He flatly refused to comment on his report, and would not even disclose where the gypsum might be found. His attitude was hard to understand, and appeared to be that his report was the property of the I.C.I. and should not be in my hands."

Not only did Goosman decline Buttle's offer of a fee to delineate the deposit, but he even refused to produce the map and key from which he had worked. The owner got round this difficulty later when an Auckland firm of surveyors prepared a grid plan of the volcano which appeared to correspond with the various features mentioned in the report.

The engineer's obstruction was strange. Buttle believed that it was due to a wish to avoid any connection with a further attempt to exploit the mineral deposits. Should such working prove successful, Goosman apparently felt he might invite criticism from the Barter Trading Corporation, which had paid for the survey. Since this company took more than a year to consider the position before deciding upon liquidation of the New Zealand Sulphur Co., his stand seems to have been rather unreasonable.

On 4 December, as if to underline Goosman's condemnation of the island, Thomson concluded his labours with the payment of a fourth and final dividend. In all the distributions amounted to 9.03d. in the pound, hardly a munificent sum. Wealth had indeed been extracted not from the mountain but from the unfortunate shareholders. These included members of the Buttle family, and the only consolation was that the liquidation had at least permitted the island to pass into their hands.

Although unable to get any co-operation from Goosman, Buttle was determined to find out more about the gypsum prospect when peace returned after World War II. He wanted to join the scientists who studied all aspects of the island in January 1947, but failed to do so because of transport limitations.

He sent details to James Healy, the volcanologist in the party,

Dolphins escort H.M.N.Z.S. *Mako* on the way to the island

The island looms grim and forbidding as *Mako* approaches the south coast. The Ohauora gannetries are white against the pohutu-kawa background.

A boat leaves for the shore. Vic Davis carries a tramping pack

Sailors from *Mako* haul the dinghy on to Bungalow Beach

who searched for the deposit, but due to a misunderstanding the latter looked for it inside the crater instead of on the outer slopes. He took photographs on the northern side of the cone, some of which showed what appeared to be the gypsum bed. Healy did not actually examine it, but from a distance thought the mineral might be white clay.

Both Healy and Dr Charles A. Fleming carefully studied the occurrence of gypsum in the crater. They came to the conclusion that not only were the deposits too small and scattered to be of economic value, but contrary to the impression given by Goosman's report the material was usually far from pure, often being blackened by the presence of iron. Samples from various locations showed gypsum percentages varying between 12.2 and 43.5%, with most around 20%.

In a subsequent paper Fleming published on the subject, *Gypsum at White Island*, he recalled Bartrum's earlier description of how gypsum was formed by the action of acidic fumes on feldspars in the volcanic rocks. It was commonly found near both live and extinct fumaroles, also in beds or layers, which consisted of material washed down by rain.

Fleming went on to point out the similarity between New Zealand and Japan in so far as gypsum was concerned. It was formed by volcanic action, and a fairly high rainfall was common to both countries. By contrast in the United States deposits usually resulted from the mineral being laid down by evaporation after the flooding of arid locations. In the latter case the gypsum was often remarkably pure, so much so that the volcanic type would find it very difficult to compete in the market.

On 22 February 1947 Buttle and Healy made a close inspection of what they believed to be Goosman's find, though without his map they could not be sure of this. A sample collected from the deposit proved on analysis to contain no gypsum at all, the material being a glassy or colloidal silica.

After this disappointment Buttle still wondered sometimes if there "might not be a worthwhile sulphur deposit tucked away somewhere." On one occasion he made a tentative enquiry about a new method of extracting the mineral from gases given off by the fumaroles, but took no further action.

Bearing in mind all the efforts which had been made, not to mention the expenditure of more than a quarter of a million pounds, without being able to establish a profitable industry, it is amusing to read a letter Buttle once received from a hopeful carpenter:

"Dear Sir,

"I understand that you are the owner of White Island. If this is so I would be pleased if you would let me know if I could rent or lease the island for a time.

"The reason for this is that a couple of mates and myself would like to prospect the land and work any minerals found there.

"If you agree to this I would be obliged if you would give me full details, especially regarding the safety of the place, as I have never been there and cannot get any information regarding it."

In his reply Buttle pointed out some of the difficulties this happy band would be certain to encounter, and closed with the firm statement,

"I am not prepared to negotiate working rights to any party unless I am well satisfied they have sufficient funds available to make success a reasonable possibility."

He experienced really cruel luck in his efforts to visit the island. One of these frustrated ventures became something of a family joke. Buttle joined *Paroto* at Tauranga, but found he would have to share a cabin with another passenger, who was unfortunately helplessly drunk. He hastened to make sure of having the top bunk.

The scow cleared the harbour entrance, but as time went on the inclement weather became worse, the seas more mountainous. Buttle gloomily watched the water growing deeper as it surged about the cabin floor in unison with the wild gyrations of the ship, and had uncomfortable visions of shipwreck, a by no means impossible event on this inhospitable coast.

Although sleep for him was impossible, his companion was by now mercifully dead to the world, sleeping off the effects of his carouse.

At last the captain decided it was useless to go any further, it being obvious that any landing at the island in these conditions was out of the question. He therefore ordered a return to the shelter of Tauranga, where *Paroto* berthed once again at the wharf. Awakened by the cessation of the wild tossing of the vessel, Buttle's cabin-mate asked drowsily:

"Is this White Island?"

As time passed the needs of the expanding population exerted an inexorable pressure on the remaining areas of indigenous forest and wildlife refuges on the mainland. Conservationists pointed out the danger that more of the country's rather limited range of unique fauna might well follow the huia and the moa on the road to extinction.

Offshore islands were often of little value for farming or other commercial purposes, usually owing to an inadequate water supply or access difficulties. The latter, of course, was a considerable advantage from the point of view of fauna and scenic preservation, so a demand arose for these to be set aside wherever possible as sanctuaries. Although no rare species inhabited White Island it still accommodated a heavy bird population and held exceptional interest in other directions. For these reasons Bernard Sladden advocated that it should be acquired for the nation.

Perhaps as a result of this agitation, one day in 1952 Buttle received a telephone call from the Commissioner of Crown Lands, Auckland, who said that he had received instructions from the Government to buy White Island. Since it meant so much to him, Buttle at once disclaimed any wish to sell. The suggestion was then put forward that it might be gazetted as a private scenic reserve under the provisions of section 6 of the Scenery Preservation Amendment Act, 1933.

The germane provisions were:

(a)   Every person is liable to a fine not exceeding one

115

hundred pounds and shall in addition be liable to pay for all damage done, and the full market value of any timber unlawfully cut or removed, who, at any time after any land becomes a reserve under the principal Act, or the gazetting of any notice under section twenty-two of the Public Works Act, 1928, describing any private land intended to be taken or acquired as a reserve,

(b)   Lights a fire on any such land: or

(c)   Without the written consent of the Minister cuts or removes any timber thereon, or unlawfully breaks, cuts, injures, or removes any or any part of any wood, tree, shrub, fern, plant, stone, mineral, or other thing of any kind: or

(d)   Without the authority of the Governor-General under section seven of the Scenery Preservation Amendment Act, 1910 or the consent of the Minister under section two of the Scenery Preservation Amendment Act, 1926, or the authority of the Minister of Internal Affairs under section thirty-one or section thirty-two of the Animals' Protection and Game Act, 1921–22, as the case may be, has in his possession or under his control or discharges any firearm while on any such land, or kills or takes any birds or any native or imported game thereon: or

(e)   Allows any cattle, horses, or other animals to trespass upon any such land: or

(f)   In any way interferes with any such land or damages the scenic or historic features thereof.

Strictly interpreted, the law would thus have prevented any-one, including the owner, from making any changes on the island. Buttle therefore applied for the Governor-General's warrant to contain a waiver exempting him and his successors in title from the stipulations of the Act. White Island eventually became a private scenic reserve on 3 December 1953.

It may be asked how effective is the protection now afforded to the island. The natural moat of uncertain-tempered sea, thirty miles wide and with little shelter against storms, is a better guarantee against marauders than any legislative action. A casual fishing party landing there can do little harm, apart possibly from letting a campfire get out of control in the pohutukawa forest.

The real problem arises from depredations upon bird life. Although in direct conflict with provision (d), the long-standing custom of three Maori tribes to go muttonbirding at the island was not immediately banned, though the depletion of stocks on the Bay of Plenty islands generally brought in its train close seasons which at one period included White Island. It was later added to the list of areas exempted from mutton-birding. Interference with the gannet population would be a more serious matter, since poaching would gravely impair the results of scientific work which has been carried out over a long period.

Raymond Buttle took no steps to develop the gypsum or other minerals before making over the property to his son, John Raymond, in 1957. At that time the new owner had not succeeded in visiting the place, his father's efforts to take him there having been frustrated by the weather or other difficulties, so that when I got to know him he had been able to see his new domain only from a mountain on the mainland.

For some years John had it in mind to renew the search for Goosman's gypsum deposit. Since the engineer had analysed the samples to determine the sulphur content, and had spent much of his time on investigating gypsum beds for six weeks, it hardly seemed possible that he could have been completely mistaken as to the nature of the material.

Raymond Buttle and Healy worked only on what they deduced to be the position of the deposit, so there was an element of doubt whether this was the right place. Goosman gave the altitude as 500 feet above sea level, thus the location could have been anywhere along that contour in the general area.

John finally had a chance to carry out an inspection on the spot in 1964, when he joined a scientific expedition led by Mr C. J. R. Robertson of the Dominion Museum. The party included

Miss Philippa Black, a geologist, who between 18 and 24 November covered the whole island and prepared a geological map.

She located a gypsum deposit to the north of Mt Ngatoro, but this would not have been economic to work. Its position did not tally with Goosman's report, and it may well be that the seam still awaits rediscovery. It could easily have been buried during the long period since 1933 by detritus washed down by the rain or wind-blown from higher areas of the cone, or by ash falls. A combination of these factors is, of course, entirely feasible.

While Goosman was quite correct in his view that an aerial ropeway could move the material cheaply to the coast, a fairly considerable outlay would be needed to provide supporting facilities such as accommodation for the staff, since the former camp has virtually disappeared. Berthing facilities would be required for shipping on the completely exposed north shore, where some form of breakwater might well be found necessary. Bearing in mind the distinctly limited cubic content of the area of the cone in question, it appears very unlikely that mineral reserves would be sufficient to justify the indicated capital costs of extraction.

John does not contemplate mineral development, but believes the island may have a future as an unusual and quite outstanding tourist attraction. In view of the uncertainty of sea communication however, this phase is likely to have to wait until helicopters or vertical take-off aircraft have been further developed to the stage where these could provide transport for visitors at a reasonable cost.

The practicability of this means of approach was amply demonstrated on 29 April 1968, when a R.N.Z.A.F. Iroquois helicopter of No. 3 Squadron, piloted by Flying Officer E. Creelman, landed a party of scientists on the crater flat. It remained there from 9 a.m. until 5.15 p.m., leaving a little earlier than planned since the volcano was in a fairly active state and a change in the direction of the wind brought the risk of ash reaching the machine. Even with a stop at Tauranga to collect additional passengers, the flight from Auckland took only two hours. A day trip to White Island for overseas tourists paying a brief visit to Auckland is therefore perfectly feasible if the problem of expense can be overcome.

A further possibility is, of course, the hovercraft, since this could enter the crater at Te Awapuia, Wilson or Shark Bays, so eliminating the time-consuming and sometimes difficult operation of landing by small boats from launches. Such a craft would probably have to be based at Tauranga rather than Auckland unless faster models are produced in the future.

John and his family prefer the sea, and in the early sixties he had a yacht built, which was named *Achernar*. In this he took a party which included scientists and some keen fishermen to White Island in December 1966, a cruise no doubt to be repeated in the years to come, since he "likes to get out to see his volcano every couple of years or so." He has fortunately not inherited the frustrations his father suffered in this connection, having achieved a much more successful record to date.

He does not lack offers from would-be buyers, several having come from Whakatane, where quite recently it was proposed to make a further attempt to exploit its "mineral riches." An Australian offered as much as $10,000 for a half share.

"I was rather surprised afterwards to think how quickly I had said 'No'," John recalled.

The uncanny fascination of the place, which still gripped Gilberd after an absence of nearly forty years, exercises just as powerful a hold on the owner's family. Raymond Buttle was perhaps if anything understating the case when he wrote:

"We would all hate to lose it." So long as White Island remains in such keeping I for one will have few qualms about its future.

VI

Way to the Island

"Land in sight, an island or rather several small ones most probably 3 Kings, so that it was conjectured that we had passed the cape which had so long troubled us. Calm most of the day: myself in a boat shooting in which I had good success, killing chiefly several gannets or Solan geese so like European ones that they are hardly distinguishable from them. As it was the humour of the ship to keep Christmas in the old fashioned way it was resolved of them to make a goose pye for tomorrow's dinner."

(24 December 1769)

"Our goose pye was eat with great approbation and in the evening all hands were as drunk as our forefathers used to be upon the like occasion."

(25 December 1769)
The Journal of Joseph Banks.

Since the menu aboard H.M.S. *Endeavour* had only recently featured shags (cormorants) shot at Mercury Bay, it is evident that the ship's company took a lively culinary interest in the passing fauna. No longer may the solan or sea goose be killed for the pot, for in New Zealand it is now a completely protected species.

As an amateur ornithologist I had known for a long time that there were gannet colonies on White Island. It was not until January 1957 when at Cape Kidnappers I met Reginald Williams, the warden of the sanctuary, that I first succumbed to the potent spell of these splendid birds, which are to be seen to advantage at the headland:

"The gannet with a wingspread of seventy inches is one

121

of the largest seabirds in New Zealand. . . . Its white plumage, with black wingtips and pastel yellow head make it a bird of outstanding beauty, and its skill as a diver cannot fail to impress the most casual observer."

Williams impressed me as being a true conservationist at heart, motivated I believe entirely by the pleasure of caring for these birds, in which task he was ably supported by a band of young enthusiasts under his leadership. The southern black-backed gull (*Larus dominicanus*) had been causing trouble by stealing and eating gannet eggs. He told me with some relish how, after securing the necessary permission from the Department of Internal Affairs, he had been thinning out the marauders with a rifle.

While more than anything else he wanted to maintain the number of his pets, he did not seem to be particularly interested in such studies as population dynamics or migratory patterns which occupied the attention of the scientists who worked at the Cape under the guidance of Dr K.A. Wodzicki, Ph.D., from Wellington. Williams weighed against the value of the knowledge gained the inevitable interference with the gannets during banding operations, and questioned its necessity.

On returning to Whakatane, I seriously considered making a start on banding and recording work in the Bay of Plenty. I discussed the possibility with my friends Messrs H.D. London and V.T. Davis, and we decided to make enquiries.

Wodzicki, then Director of the Animal Ecology Division of the Department of Scientific and Industrial Research, had worked not only at Cape Kidnappers but, with the late Rev. F.H. Robertson, at White Island also in 1947 and 1949. At the latter they had the earlier observations of Dr W.R.B. Oliver in 1912, and Bernard Sladden in 1925–36 to guide them.

The Ornithological Society of New Zealand organised a census of the Australasian gannet (*Sula serrator*) throughout the country during the 1946–7 breeding season. Prior to this no accurate count of the White Island population had been made, and unless such statistics are recorded from time to time over a period of years it is, of course, impossible to tell either the rate or extent that the colonies may be increasing or decreasing in numbers. Important field work, supplemented by aerial photographs, was accomplished in 1947, and an expedition organised by the D.S.I.R. in November 1949 gave the opportunity to follow up the preliminary investigations. There had since been a lapse of some years, so my friends and I proposed to attempt at least one visit.

It was, we knew only too well, one thing to decide to go to the island, but actually getting there was quite another matter. One woman I met told me that she had been trying unsuccessfully for fourteen years. In the first place the distance the island lay offshore greatly restricted the number of craft then available at Whakatane or Tauranga which were suitable for the trip. In the case of a launch carrying fare-paying passengers, the Marine Department quite rightly set standards of seaworthiness and life-saving equipment to give the best possible protection.

This meant that a fairly large party had to be assembled to cover the cost of chartering a launch which met these requirements, involving in turn hiring a bus for transport to and from Tauranga, since there was no such vessel at Whakatane. More than one useless journey of more than fifty miles each way had been made, only to find on arrival that the weather was thought unsuitable for putting to sea. White Island is too small and exposed to provide any worthwhile shelter if conditions are bad, nor is the Bay of Plenty coast blessed with good harbours.

On one occasion a party which included Mr V.T. (Vic) Davis had sailed from Tauranga in the *Tidesong*. A few people were able to land at Crater Bay, but the weather deteriorated and for some hours it seemed likely that they might be marooned. Vic eventually managed to take them off by dinghy from a rock shelf which, although he did not know it at the time, had been used by a party of officers who landed from H.M.S. *Diomede* in the days of White Island Products. For this reason it was afterwards called the Diomede Rock. So far as Vic was concerned it was a case of so near and yet so far, for on this

123

occasion he did not actually set foot ashore during the rescue operation. Some of his companions were seasick for the whole thirteen hours of the trip.

In their escape these would-be maroons were as fortunate as their Maori predecessors though its mode, not lacking in excitement, was certainly less dramatic. Te Tawhero Tuiti (the late Albert O. Stewart of Whakatane) has related the story of the better-known of these exiles:

"Long ago there lived Te Tahi-o-te-Rangi. Now Te Tahi was a tohunga of high standing, reputed to possess supernatural powers and to be an adept at witchcraft and other secret arts known only to tohungas. He became, however, very unpopular with the tribes with whom he lived because he was suspected of using his powers for sinister purposes. He was a member of the Ngatiawa tribes who were living at Whare-o-Toroa pa, better known as Whakatane pa.

"Now this suspicion of him having become so great amongst the people, that when on a certain season their kumara crops became blighted, they attributed this disaster to Te Tahi's witchcraft, because he had resented his unpopularity.

"During Te Tahi's absence from the pa on one occasion, the people held a secret meeting and decided that there was no doubt about Te Tahi's guilt, and passed a verdict that he was to be done away with. However, as no one was found daring enough to kill him, it was decided to take him to White Island and leave him there to perish.

"In order to carry out this scheme, he was invited to go with a fishing expedition. Now amongst Te Tahi's many accomplishments was his superior knowledge of the best fishing grounds, and this was made as the special reason why he should go with the expedition. In due course a large number of canoes forming the expedition voyaged out to sea, and made straight for White Island where the best fishing grounds were to be found. They landed on the island and prepared to camp there.

124

"In order to get rid of Te Tahi for a while, he was sent to fetch water, which was a good way from the camp and round a promontory. No sooner did he disappear around this point than the canoes were launched and everybody left, leaving poor old Te Tahi behind. On his return, he found no one in camp, and he saw the canoes a good way off the island making straight for the mainland; and then he knew that he was deliberately left behind to perish. He sat down on the rocks near the edge of the water and wept, and to this day that spot is known as 'Te Tahi's Rock.'

"Not long afterwards, however, he noticed a disturbance in the water, and looking closely he beheld denizens of the deep cruising around just below him, and amongst them he noticed a whale, large in size. It suddenly dawned on him that they were taniwhas and that he held sway over them by virtue of his supernatural powers. Thereupon he called to the whale which was named Tutarakauika and, as it rose to the surface of the water alongside the rock, Te Tahi stepped on its back. . . . Because the whale was of the supernatural species it conveyed to Te Tahi, by some means or other, its desire to know whether or not he wanted the canoes and their occupants destroyed. Te Tahi briefly replied, 'Waiho ma te whakama e patu.' (Let shame be their punishment.)

"We are told that Te Tahi and his whale circled well away from the canoes so that they might not be seen. He landed on a rock known as the 'Rukupo,' a small rock which becomes fully submerged at high tide and lying directly off the Kohi Point. From there he reached the mainland and walked along the rocks till he reached the sandy beach below the Harbour Board's signal station.

"By then the canoes were just approaching the mouth of the Whakatane River, and some of the occupants remarked at the close resemblance to Te Tahi of the person walking on the beach. When, however, the canoes entered the narrows, they came within close proximity of the pedestrian on the shore, and then it was they became thunderstruck to find it was none other than Te Tahi himself. To make

125

doubly sure, they hailed him and asked if he were Te Tahi, and he replied in the affirmative with a wave of the hand. Te Tahi then had the satisfaction of seeing them hang their heads in shame."

After such an experience at the hands of his own people, the tohunga felt there was little prospect of future happiness in their midst. He had received far kinder treatment from the taniwha, and he resolved to become one himself, which he did upon diving into the Whakatane River at a spot afterwards known as Te Ana-o-Te Tahi (the home of Te Tahi). He subsequently devoted his powers to helping those in difficulties at sea, and when a Maori fisherman of Maketu was later marooned at Whakaari for an infringement of the law of tapu, Te Tahi brought him safely home.

While Te Tahi's supernatural allies were obviously in a class of their own, the island none the less does seem to attract unusual creatures of the sea albeit, unfortunately, the dead and the dying.

During one of John Buttle's visits an unusual skull was picked up, which appeared to him to be that of a dolphin. It was later identified as belonging to a male specimen of the beaked whale. This genus, Mesoplodon, is generally found in tropical waters. It was the only specimen recorded at that time as being recovered in temperate areas of the western Pacific, though four female skulls had previously been washed ashore in Japan.

Another visitor, the paper nautilus (*Argonauta nodosa*), is a member of the octopus family. Although nothing like so uncommon as the beaked whale, for indeed on occasion these molluscs have been seen in large numbers, it is never the less of considerable interest. The female, while conforming to the accepted physique of the cephalopod, has the distinction of carrying a delicately beautiful white shell in which to secrete her eggs. This is so fragile that when cast up on an inhospitable shore damage is almost inevitable.

Few landfalls could be more forbidding to such a creature

than the cliffs and boulder beaches of White Island, and it is fortunate that on Labour Day, 1932 Albert Mokomoko happened to arrive on a visit which coincided with a wholesale invasion by the paper nautilus. One of his passengers was a Mr Graham, father of the late David H. Graham, a foremost authority on New Zealand marine life. He noted his impressions for his son of this remarkable occurrence:

"There were thousands of paper nautilus within sight all along the coast, where there was no shelving beach, only rocks. The waves were dashing them in amongst the rocks, smashing them to pieces, causing the animals to swim to safety as the seagulls were swooping down on them, flying up in the air and dropping them on the rocks; then flying down and picking up the broken pieces of the octopod.

"The shoreline was white with thousands of broken or whole paper nautilus and one could not walk without treading on them. Every shell I examined had eggs which were in the smallest part, and of a creamy white colour. Upon picking up a shell complete with animal and giving the shell a sharp jerk, the animal fell out and either swam away like an octopus or crawled out of sight among the rocks. When I put my finger alongside the head of the animal, it would give a sharp bite similar to that of a mouse.

"Upon enquiring of Albert Mokomoko, a frequent visitor to the island for the twenty years preceding 1932, he said that he had never seen these shells before. . . . Some of the party took a dinghy and rowed round to the other side of the island and saw quite as many shells all along the coastline."

The shell is carried only by the female, who is able to form a new one if the original is damaged or lost.

Some thirty-two years later, very opportunely when Robertson's team of skilled observers happened to be present in the latter part of November, there was a similar stranding all along the shore of paper nautilus in vast numbers. Whether or not October and November are months when such an in-

127

vasion is particularly likely is not known, nor is the reason for this strange occurrence.

To return to our proposed visit, it was evident that cumbersome ventures involving large parties would be unsuitable, being not only time-consuming but also because the presence of too many people would hinder us. We therefore sought a smaller craft at Whakatane. Mr H.D. (Jack) London seemed to be associated in one way or another with most of the deserving causes in the district, and as a result had a wide circle of friends. One of these was Tom Fuller, the headmaster of Allandale School, who had a launch capable of taking four people to the island, and he agreed to help us.

Our plans received immediate encouragement from Dr Wodzicki, Mr H.R. McKenzie, doyen of the Ornithological Society, also his colleague, Mr P.A.S. Stein. The latter had been engaged in research dealing with the life-cycle and other aspects of the gannet at Horuhoru, an islet in the Hauraki Gulf fairly near his holiday home on Waiheke Island. His results were outstanding, as may be gathered from part of an article he contributed to the *Proceedings of the New Zealand Ecological Society:*

"Three years were spent on counting eggs and chicks as often as once a week, to determine mortality; dozens of eggs were marked and numbered to find the incubation period, and all known chicks were measured to get an idea of their rate of growth, and their feathering cycle. We found that adult gannets spend six or seven months of the year in active work at their rookery. Upwards of a month was spent in preparing a nest, and laying one egg. Both birds shared hatching duties for at least 43 days. Most eggs hatched in between 43 and 43½ days and any egg unhatched after 44 days was found to be addled or to contain a fully mature chick that had died in hatching. Up to 97% of the eggs hatched but in a bad season up to 86% of the chicks died, leaving as few as 250 (from over 1,500 nests) to fly away."

In view of this very high mortality among chicks Stein formed

One of *Mako's* crew tries his hand at banding a gannet held in the catcher by the author

Landing at Crater Bay

The crater in a fairly active phase, c.1930
Steam and smoke billowing from Big Donald, named after Donald
Pye, the fireman whose body was never found

the opinion that it might take twenty years for a breeding pair to successfully rear two young birds to replace themselves. He told me of a subsequent calculation made on a computer which estimated the time required to be twenty-three years so if, as is believed, the New Zealand gannet population is slowly increasing, it follows that the species must be a long lived one.

It was, of course, necessary for us to secure the owner's permission to land at White Island. John Buttle had previously lent me material for a nature exhibition staged by the Whakatane section of the Royal Forest and Bird Protection Society, and so was no stranger. In reply to my application he not only expressed his warm approval of the project, but also the hope that on some future occasion he might join us.

Preparations were finally completed and at 3 a.m. on 6 December, 1958 shadowy figures were stowing the last of a miscellaneous cargo aboard the launch *Iolanthe* at the Whakatane waterfront. Casting off, we put on a burst of speed to carry the boat through the confused surf at the notorious harbour bar, where a number of vessels have come to grief from time to time.

As we drew away from the land the rising sun began to light up the heavy cloud over the Kaimanawa Range away to the east. Conditions were far from ideal, for there was an easterly swell, and a rising wind brought with it a breaking sea.

Whale Island dropped astern, and as we sat huddled in warm clothing, speculating on the steadily receding prospects of being able to land at White Island, there was a call from the helmsman:

"Your rudder's gone!"

He spun the wheel to prove it. We were twenty miles offshore, with no radio, and the launch suddenly seemed very small on the heaving grey sea. The owner located the cause of the trouble almost at once. The rudder was fortunately intact, but the rusted steering cable had parted, probably under the strain of keeping the craft on its course in a beam sea.

A solution of our trouble was not difficult. Tom's main interest in the trip was fishing, and there was a gaff in the boat.

129

The steering cable had operated a wheel mounted on the rudder-post. The gaff, worked in between the spokes and firmly lashed in place, made a serviceable tiller. Despite the mishap, nobody had any thought of making for home; all eyes turned once more to the sombre hulk of the volcano ahead. Our luck, in fact, seemed to be changing, for the wind and choppy sea began to go down quite noticeably, and an occasional patch of blue showed in the leaden sky.

There was now another splash of colour to enliven the greyness. A long plume of steam drifting across the sea from White Island is usually part of the Bay of Plenty scene, but before us rose a towering column of what appeared to be brown smoke. We thought it was more likely to be a new shower of ash, which is often of that colour, and hoped it would not prevent us from going into the crater. When *Iolanthe* was within a mile or two of the south coast the billowing vapour gradually lightened in tone to a rose pink, and we decided that it must after all be steam and not smoke.

Although the island is not very high, for Mt Gisborne is only 1,053 feet, the peak falls very sharply to the sea. The small concrete dam, built thirty years before, was in a perfect state of preservation, though blackened by time. It appeared to be no more than a child's plaything on those grim scoria slopes. Ahead of us reared the Club Rocks, craggy and inhospitable except to seabirds. Our approach to these stacks was noted by the white-fronted terns (*Sterna striata*) which breed there. These birds came diving and wheeling over the launch with melancholy cries. They had nothing to fear, however, for we were bound for Te Awapuia, or Crater Bay, the largest of the three places where the cone has completely disappeared.

I was at the helm as the launch entered the bay, and the scene was nothing if not dramatic. Straight ahead of us stood a precipitous peak, Troup Head. Sheltering immediately beneath this giant mass were the roofless ruins of the old factory buildings, whose mute tribute to the vain efforts of man to come to terms with this hostile environment was underlined by the concrete jetty, broken at the landward end, so that it lurched down at an angle to the water. As the whole expanse of the crater came into view, steam rose high into the now bright morning sunshine. We were able to strip off parkas and pullovers to land in summer clothes.

Although *Iolanthe* drew little water, Tom would not risk damage to the hull by going in to what was by courtesy termed the beach, and I circled slowly round the bay while the others prepared to lower the dinghy. We anchored and then set about landing. If the launch was small, its tender was a cockleshell indeed. I for one secretly (and devoutly) hoped it would never be called upon to serve as a lifeboat. Eventually the four of us, with cameras and other equipment, were ferried ashore.

There was a short expanse of sand, but this was much encumbered by large water-worn boulders and driftwood, so that care was needed to choose a suitable spot to pull the boat clear of the sea, which by now was almost calm. At the head of the beach stood a low ridge; John Buttle later told me this was composed of gypsum. There was a gap in it not far from the jetty, where the bed of a stream, then dry, broke through.

In wet weather the crater collects the rainfall like a giant saucer. Some of it, of course, enters the blowholes and appears to cause an increased output of steam for a short time afterwards. The greater part is collected by numerous small channels it has formed over the years in the soft ground, to feed what is known as the acid stream. This discharges into the sea at Te Awapuia, sometimes noticeably discolouring the bay. The flow contains acids from the mineral salts which the rainwater dissolves on its passage through the crater. Red-billed gulls (*Larus scopulinus*), which at times nest near the stream and bathe in it, have been seen with feathers so burned that little but the shafts remained.

The old factory was our first objective, but even before we reached it there was evidence of previous human occupation, the skeleton of what had once been a Model T Ford truck sinking into the ground. It could easily be identified by the very slim rear axle, more recognisable than the engine. The sump of the latter had been removed, the exposed crankshaft and connecting rods being nothing but a mass of corroded metal. Nearby lay the mobile drilling platform, strongly built in wood which, apart from its solid rubber tyres, had stood up well to the attacks of fumes and weather. Gilberd later told me with a smile that the tyres were not in very good shape even when he left the island.

We then went inside the factory, if such an expression can be used in the case of a roofless building. The Oregon pine of the roof trusses was still in excellent condition, and indeed one man in Whakatane had plans to remove it. The securing bolts, however, were badly corroded, and the asbestos cladding lay in fragments strewn over the concrete floor. Although one face of the tall fertiliser hoppers had collapsed outwards, the walls generally had stood the test of time well. In one corner was stacked what had been listed at the time of the liquidation as "eleven tons of cement, gone hard." Twenty-five years later it was certainly that, perfectly shaped from the bags which had long since disappeared.

Most of the plant and machinery had been removed from the building. One of the most valuable items, the 72 h.p. Tangye engine, did duty for some years at a lime works near Whangarei. The most striking piece of plant remaining was the rotary drier. Gilberd said that this had not been particularly efficient in use, and its size may have discouraged any attempt to dismantle and ship it to the mainland. The Fordson tractor was still there, though without its front-end loader. Its solid tyres reminded me of the days of my childhood, when even buses were so equipped. Part of the steering wheel was missing, and little remained of the radiator core.

The effect upon metal of the crater atmosphere, reinforced by salt from the sea only a few yards away, had to be seen to be fully appreciated. It was most graphically illustrated in the case of the portable boiler. This vehicle was fitted with cast-iron wheels, the spokes being about two inches thick. In the left rear wheel these were completely eate 1 through, with the result that the axle had collapsed on the floor. Pieces of solid iron more than a quarter of an inch thick could be broken off with the fingers, and snapped like a biscuit.

It was depressing to gaze upon the ruin not only of the plant and buildings but also the bright hopes of so many people. We moved to the west and with a sense of relief turned our backs on the dead enterprise to face the roaring steam as we walked up Crater Flat. The hummocks left by the 1914 lahar were still prominent. The floor of the crater proved to be largely a hot mud, none too comfortable to feet protected only by sandshoes, for at times we would sink ankle deep into the surface at every step.

The first feature to attract our attention was the Donald Mound. This was close to the site of the former blowhole known as Big Donald, which disappeared before 1949. It was coloured green and yellow due to the presence of mineral salts, and was steaming vigorously. The molten rock is believed to be close to the surface at this point, where Mr G.E.K. Thompson recorded a temperature of 580°C. in January, 1955.

The roar of escaping steam was quite nerve-racking. Vic asked me to pose in the act of looking at the mound while he took a photograph from behind me. I stood there for what seemed a long time until Jack came up and tapped me on the shoulder. They had been shouting, but no whisper reached me in the overpowering clamour.

We were astonished by the colour to be found on slopes clear of the mud. In one place the concentration of pellets of various salts was quite dazzling even when seen through sunglasses, and we dubbed it the "Flower Garden", for it bore more than a passing resemblance to an ornamental bed in a city park. Fumaroles were depositing needle sulphur, and there were plenty of yellow patches on the crater walls, perhaps due to the presence of iron pyrites.

Ahead of us lay the western plateau, or Crater Ridge, at the foot of which was the depression found by Goosman in 1933 immediately after the eruption. It now held a small lake, the surface golden with sulphur. A sheer cliff walled in the western shore, with a big vent discharging steam which was transparent until it had risen about ten feet in the air.

133

The crater's set-piece attracted us like a magnet. This was Noisy Nellie (who was the unfortunate lady so grossly maligned?), then the largest blowhole in the country. It was about 80 feet deep by 50 feet wide, and the huge column of steam billowed out of the ground near the base of the west wall. Apart from one or two sulphur-coloured spots, the surface of the great pit glowed with the same rose pink as the steam, which later in the day changed colour yet again, becoming white. The vent was ejecting dust and a few pebbles into the air. Jack tried throwing down a few pieces of rock to see if these would be tossed out again, but the monster treated such levity with fitting contempt.

After Noisy Nellie any other volcanic feature would have seemed an anticlimax. My companions were complaining of headaches from the fumes, so we returned to our dinghy. Rowing out from the shore was like escaping from some inferno, and we soon refreshed ourselves in the clean sea air.

It was pleasant at our anchorage on the sparkling waters of Crater Bay, and before moving round to Ohauora we settled down in *Iolanthe* to enjoy the warm sunshine and a picnic lunch. It seems scarcely credible, but when jam was brought out we were soon joined by some of the comparatively few winged insects which inhabit the island, in this case the little native bee (*Paracolletes boltoni*).

After lunch we left Te Awapuia, and the launch hugged the southern coast as it passed below the great cliff of Gannet Point, where the white birds soared high over our heads as they went to and fro on their family chores. Although Tom had accompanied us on our tour of the crater he thought it advisable to remain on board *Iolanthe* when we halted off Rocky Point, a sinister but well-merited name.

Jack, Vic and I therefore made our way gingerly ashore on to the smooth-faced wet black boulders of Bungalow Beach, with never a vestige of sand. Here we soon came upon the first traces of the former settlement, for the tall samson post of the camp derrick still stood erect as a lonely sentinel, with the rusted remains of the winch at its foot. A pathway, flanked on one side by a hedge-like growth of taupata, led past the Ohauora "a" gannetry to the ruins of what was once the guest house.

It was hard to visualise how it had looked in the days when it knew the excited chatter and laughter of the Gilberd children. They had certainly enjoyed a grandstand view of the nesting site, which reached almost to their doors. They referred to the colony (and still do) as the "gannet patch", the term used by the sulphur workers. Peter Stein prefers the old English "rookery" to the more modern word "gannetry", so there is quite a variety of names for a single object.

The nests took the shape of a flattened cone with a central hollow, resembling miniature volcanoes. These were distributed over most of the gently sloping site, being spaced about thirty inches apart to permit birds at a nest to gain some respite from pecking by their neighbours while there, though such attacks were common enough when they passed through the colony.

This was necessary because the site was too flat for a gannet to fly off from a standing start, as it could on a steep slope. In this case a bird had to make its way to the pathway we had just ascended, and there begin to run down the slight gradient towards the sea. These fine seabirds had no superior when in flight, but were absurdly clumsy as they shambled awkwardly over the ground with wings flapping for the take-off.

There was a constant coming and going of adult birds as they cared for and fed their young. While one parent stood guard over the chick its mate would set out on the endless round of fishing. Although this was generally carried out at some distance from the island, we saw instances of the spectacular manner in which a bird, on sighting a fish swimming below, would clap its wings to its body and plunge into the sea like a torpedo.

Upon returning home, the incoming bird went through a peculiar style of greeting with its partner. This took the form of rubbing heads and bills up and down each other's necks. It could be either a display of affection, or designed to assist the newcomer to regurgitate its catch of fish, possibly both.

135

The hungry chick took the earliest opportunity to thrust its bill into the parent's wide-open beak for a feed. The former guardian at the nest would then leave on a fishing trip, to be replaced by its tired partner.

Being conscious of our time slipping away, we struck off across the shallow gully which divided the two sections of the Ohauora colony and entered the forest, making for the main campsite. There was no undergrowth to hinder us, but the muttonbird burrows frequently gave way under us as we walked over the soft ground, so that our progress was punctuated by feet suddenly sinking through the surface. Later in the day we saw a launch near West Point, and it seemed the area we were crossing had been hunted quite thoroughly, for no young birds protested at our involuntary destruction of their homes.

The next building we came upon was Gilberd's former cottage. Its iron roof had gone, probably removed by some casual visitor who could find a use for it at home. The timber walls of the two rooms and verandah were still there, also the concrete fireplace. The structure had resisted the ravages of time better than the rest of the living quarters. Some of these buildings leaned at crazy angles, others had collapsed altogether, and it seemed that a certain amount of material had either been removed or used to feed muttonbirders' fires. It was a sad contrast with the neat little settlement we knew from old photographs.

As we emerged from the forest at the Ohauora "c" gannet colony a more enduring relic came to light. This was the concrete pit containing the foundations of the condensing plant for distilling sea water, though it might easily have been overlooked since it was largely hidden by a later growth of taupata. The original housing built of corrugated iron had disappeared.

We observed and photographed the colony, which did not completely fill the open space above the beach. The occasional fallen trunk of some long-dead tree indicated that the forest had given ground to the gannets, and indeed some were then nesting under the fringe of the pohutukawas. The birds were in a much shyer state than those at Ohauora "a" and "b", being easily disturbed by our approach. This nervousness, coupled with the absence of chicks at the nests, smacked strongly of interference and perhaps poaching by earlier visitors.

Our day had been both long and strenuous, so upon hearing that Vic and I now proposed to start climbing the slopes of the mountain Jack not unreasonably preferred to return to *Iolanthe* rather than accompany us. We were aiming to reach the low point on the crater rim overlooking the 1914 rock slide at the western end of the crater. At this spot the cone is only about 620 feet high, and once clear of the forest we could head directly for our destination. The scattered pohutukawa scrub on the open slope was no hindrance, but loose stones, combined with the steep angle of climb, discouraged any undue haste.

On looking down to the coast we were able to observe a phenomenon at the Ohauora gannetries. From where we stood a blue haze could be clearly seen, looking exactly like smoke from a wood fire, drifting above the trees, but we knew there was nobody in the area at the time. This peculiarity was noticed by Walsh in 1930, and is believed to be due to hydrochloric acid in fumes from the crater combining with ammonia derived from the excrement of the birds to produce ammonium chloride.

When we reached the crater rim we found that much of the material forming it was a dried mud, most probably from ash. This was extremely brittle, and gave way at every touch. We therefore exercised a good deal of care not to be literally carried away during our photographic exercises here. The view below was certainly well worth the effort of the climb even in our tired state, being far more impressive when the whole panorama could be taken in at a glance rather than viewed piecemeal as it was bound to be if walking over the crater flat.

Upon returning to *Iolanthe* we held a council of war. It had originally been our intention to stay at the island overnight to allow further exploration the next day. Although we had seen nothing of the north coast, we felt much had been achieved by this reconnaissance, and as the weather was an uncertain factor it seemed a wise plan to start the trip home while conditions were good.

Tom first wanted to go to a spot he fancied close to the Volkner Rocks for an hour or two's fishing, so we set off westward and rounded the promontory beyond Poroporo, possibly the one which figured in Te Tahi's story. A deserted launch lay close to the foot of Te Hokowhitu gully, her complement evidently being ashore muttonbirding. The pohutukawas here were the best on the island, the forest clothing the slopes rising to the magnificent ridge over 600 feet high linking Mt Ngatoro to the abrupt cliff of the north-west coast. The tops of the trees on the crest were quite noticeably dust-covered by ash from the volcano.

Te Matawiwi (West Point) was one of the finest sights we saw on an island which can justly claim to be scenically well-endowed. About 200 feet above the sea the forest gave way to open ground. Much of this was covered with a vivid green carpet of mesembryanthemum (*Disphyma australe*) showing up the scattered white gannet colonies in startling contrast. The cliff, about 100 feet high, was so deeply undercut by the waves as to give the appearance of shallow caves at its base.

When we left Te Matawiwi astern, the great north-western cliff-face came into view. This, including Mt Ngatoro, the Club and Volkner Rocks formed part of the original volcano. We chugged slowly across the three miles or so of sea which now occupied the site of the first crater, and it was borne upon us how much greater the island was in those far-off times.

We were still more impressed by the Volkner Rocks at close quarters, for these rose tall and stark so high above the waves that we had to bend our heads backwards to gaze up at the tops of the islets. Surely the modest German priest could never have envisaged that his martyrdom would be honoured by such an impressive memorial.

Once again we were greeted by birds who had claimed the lofty tops of the rock stacks for their breeding colonies. White-fronted terns and red-billed gulls nested there in hundreds.

Modern feats of rock-climbing, such as the conquest of the Old Man of Hoy in the Orkney Islands, make one hesitate to be dogmatic as to what may or may not be inaccessible. It would, however, be a fitting test for any mountaineer to scale these walls, since even to get ashore at all is no simple matter with the constant surging of the open sea.

If human intruders from below were unlikely to disturb the peace of the nesting birds, they could still come from above. Shortly after our visit the R.N.Z.A.F. chose the islets as a target for simulated bombing practice, but the aircraft were unlikely to fly low enough to upset the sitting tenants.

The spot Tom had chosen for fishing was only a chain or two from the rocks. The water was deeper than might have been expected so close to land, for we found it necessary to tie two lines together to reach the bottom. With four fishermen in the well of the launch, the confined space was apt to become much encumbered with wet line whenever someone hopefully hauled it in.

I, of course, defended my title as one of the world's worst anglers, and could do no better than to hook some revolting eel-like creature. Perhaps as a result of the baleful glare it gave me I vomited briefly over the gunwale, to the huge amusement of my companions. Rather to their disappointment I felt perfectly well both before and afterwards, so their helpful comments on greasy salt pork and the like failed to have the desired effect.

At last my fishing friends had had their fill, and the evening shadow cast by the Volkner Rocks began to chill. *Iolanthe* got under way for the distant shore, which seemed very remote from our small, lonely craft in the gathering dusk. Having forsworn the evening meal as a precautionary measure, I was unanimously voted helmsman while the other three fed themselves and passed pleasantries at my expense. There was, unfortunately, no handy rock I could ram to shake the complacency of this self-satisfied trio.

Our navigation was devoid of such niceties as a compass, so I steered for the peak of Whale Island until it faded and was finally lost in the darkness. By then the lights of even the smaller settlements along the coast threw up a glow in the night sky, and while there was no friendly lighthouse beam to guide us, Whakatane's position could be seen at a glance.

Jack made no pretensions to being anything but a landlubber; with this very convenient excuse he turned in for the night, leaving us to it. On being relieved at the tiller I followed him into the cabin, to fall fast asleep almost at once. Only minutes later, or so it seemed, I was wide awake again. The engine had stopped, an event which has never failed to rouse me instantly during the scores of thousands of miles I travelled on the sea before renouncing it for the air.

The reason was soon evident. Vic, as an engineer, cannot bear any form of mechanical contrivance to work in any way short of perfection. Our venerable Ford motor was never again likely to achieve that glorious state, but he had stopped it in the hope of being able to improve its somewhat sluggish performance. After tinkering for a while he restarted the engine and I my interrupted sleep.

Once again, after an apparently short interval, although in fact it was about midnight, I was disturbed as *Iolanthe* came to rest in McEwen's Bay on the south coast of Whale Island. We had covered most of the distance from the Volkner Rocks, being now only about seven miles from home. It was proposed to spend the rest of the night here so that we could enter the Whakatane River in daylight.

The weird melancholy cries of the muttonbirds quite failed to keep any of us awake any longer. Early on Sunday we came into harbour with the dawn, and so completed a trip which will live long in my memory. I later gave a talk about it on the radio from 1YZ, Rotorua, and contributed an illustrated article to the *New Zealand Herald*, which was featured on the leader page.

VII

Naval and Legal Occasions

Kazimierz Wodzicki and his colleague, Rowley Taylor, who later went to Antarctica, spent a weekend with me at Whakatane during August, 1959. The primary object of their visit was to gather full information about the unexpected discovery of a colony of the rare short-tailed bat (*Mystacops tuberculatus*) by local naturalists at Matahina, not far from the site of the present power station. We took the opportunity to compare notes about White Island and the possibility of including its colonies in the gannet banding scheme.

Wodzicki was quite willing to recommend my appointment as a banding operator by the Dominion Museum, since he thought it desirable to have someone working at a point about midway between Stein at Horuhoru and himself at Cape Kidnappers. There was always, of course, the old stumbling block of transport, but he mentioned a Government vessel engaged on oceanographical survey work which might be able to be of some assistance in this direction. It was rather an outside chance, and upon his return to Wellington he found the ship was unlikely to be in the Bay of Plenty at the time we should need it. Another possibility we considered was the fisheries research vessel *Ikatere*, which had previously visited White Island, but here once again schedules of duties did not happen to coincide with our requirements.

The Navy appeared to me to be a far better prospect. It had a small squadron of fishery protection motor launches, one of which was detailed each year to carry out what was commonly known as the muttonbird patrol in the Bay of Plenty for a week or more during November. A wildlife ranger from the Department of Internal Affairs was then taken to the various islands to keep a check upon the activities of parties hunting the young of the grey-faced petrel (*Pterodroma macroptera*).

This particular period was ideally suited to banding gannets, since the work can best be carried out during November and December. The great majority of the chicks have by then grown big enough to avoid the risk of the numbered band slipping off over the foot when the latter is drawn up by the bird, but at the same time feathering is not sufficiently advanced for the young to be able to fly away from the colonies.

One of the duties of the fishery patrol launches was to take scientists to the offshore islands for study purposes. I certainly cannot claim to be one of these highly intelligent and dedicated people whose work is too often not sufficiently appreciated by the general public. On the other hand our little group might, with some official recognition and encouragement, be able to carry out field work which would provide information not otherwise available to the various scientific departments.

I felt it best to go straight to the top when approaching the Navy. Since we had established contact with Wodzicki at the D.S.I.R., I took his name in vain when writing to the Navy Secretary in Wellington. The response was favourable, and in due course the Naval Officer in Charge, Auckland (Commodore L.P.Bourke) placed H.M.N.Z.S. *Mako* at our disposal. It was not everyone, we thought, who was so provided with one of Her Majesty's ships, complete with crew, even though the main armament did consist of no more than two .303 rifles, supplemented by the captain's revolver.

In addition to this vital link in the chain, Mr F.C.Kinsky, Banding Convenor at the Dominion Museum, approved my appointment. He produced not only the schedules and bands for use at the colonies, but also added his expert advice to Wodzicki's.

It was originally proposed that we should use the wharf at Ohiwa Harbour as our point of embarkation, but the weather was initially unfavourable, so eventually *Mako* spent the night of 21–22 November anchored at Whale Island prior to picking us up at dawn from Ohope Beach.

Vic lived very conveniently at the west end of the beach,

so we spent the night at his house. Our team consisted of Jack, Vic and myself from the previous year, also a newcomer in the person of Herbert Grubner, whose equal as a knowledgeable amateur naturalist I have seldom met. Vic and I shared a front bedroom, and when the alarm woke us in the small hours of the morning, I looked out to sea.

"She's on her way," I reported.

Mako's lights were bright, but the launch was still a long way off. The front rooms of the house were lit by fluorescent tubes, which we switched on, so that with the curtains drawn back a beacon blazed from the darkness of the sleeping waterfront to guide *Mako*. Her captain, Lieut J.H. Cole, D.S.C., R.N.Z.N., would at least know we were up and about.

By 3.30 a.m., well loaded down with packs and other equipment, we were making our way across the hard wet sand, for it was nearly low tide. The silhouette of the launch against the greying sky showed that she was now as close in to the shore as it was prudent to come, and a signal lamp suddenly stabbed a message across the dark waters. Both Vic and I had learned the Morse code during Navy days in World War II, but that was a long time ago, and our memories were no longer up to reading it.

Its meaning was soon obvious, for instead of putting off a boat to pick us up from the beach *Mako* headed westwards for the headland which walls off Ohope from Otarawairere Bay. At its base were flat rocks from which the dinghy was able to collect us instead of having to make repeated trips through the breakers, so we were able to arrive on board dry shod.

The launch was fairly compact, and we passed our time either on the bridge or in the wheelhouse, which accommodated the radar screen. The latter, however, held little of interest after we drew away from the land. We came abreast of Whale Island, lying well to the west of our course, and as it fell astern we watched the familiar white patches which marked the gannet colonies on White Island grow steadily larger.

It was nearly six o'clock when the captain suddenly came down into the wheelhouse and peered at the radar screen. A small white mark appeared about midway between ourselves and the land ahead of us, and was taken to be a boat leaving White Island. As we carried on along our course the other vessel gradually came plainly into view, towing a dinghy in her wake. She proved to be the *Aio* out of Opotiki, carrying a party of fifteen Maoris who had been on a muttonbirding expedition.

Lieut Cole was an honorary wildlife ranger, and decided to inspect their take of birds, so as the launch approached us he hailed her with an order to stop. Although *Mako* was flying the white ensign at the time, and a merchant vessel was therefore legally bound to obey any orders given by her commander, the *Aio* reduced speed to slow and described a wide circle in the calm sea without actually coming to a halt. Cole tried to bring his ship alongside her, but manoeuvring at low speed with little steerage way was difficult, and at one point he had to take quick action to avert a collision.

He intended to retire from the Navy in the near future, and had no desire to spoil his record with a possible claim for damage if he rammed the other craft. It was evident that the *Aio* would not stop, which was in itself suspicious, but he did not wish to delay us, so he waved her on her way, being rewarded with an ironic salute from the helmsman. The muttonbirding party had managed to evade an inspection of their bag, but in another direction their conduct was less circumspect. All of them were on deck in the morning sunshine, gazing at the apparently discomfited *Mako*. We responded by using two or three cameras to record their collective beauty for future reference.

The incident gave us something to talk about, but in the meantime we had the dolphins to watch. They turned up to put on their usual wonderful swimming display, and one never tires of seeing their antics. The launch could travel at about fourteen knots, but they were able to outdistance it with ease. *Mako* ran close in under the western end of the Club Rocks, standing sheer out of the sea, which were fairly fully tenanted by the nesting terns. These flew over our heads, their cries

Tom Fuller looks at the portable boiler

Noisy Nellie blows pink steam beyond the mounds left by the 1914 lahar

"The roar of escaping steam was quite nerve-racking." The Donald Mound in 1958

Mineral salts in the "Flower Garden", 1958

leaving us in little doubt that our intrusion was no more welcome than before.

Mako lost way as she came up to a position not far from Rocky Point. Not unreasonably, Cole had no intention of anchoring. The generous coating of large boulders on Bungalow Beach extended under the water, so if an anchor was let go it might easily become jammed as the vessel drifted with the tide and thus be found impossible to raise. In addition to this he had an excellent sea fishing rod with which he hoped to pass his day profitably. After landing us the launch stood out to sea, and we were on our own.

Before setting to work at the gannet colonies, we felt a walk to the old campsite might be desirable. We left our gear near the landing place, apart from cameras, and made our way through the pohutukawas. It did not take long to reach the spot where our friends of the *Aio* had spent the night, and we looked round to see if it could shed any light upon their reluctance to receive a call from a ranger. It did. Within a few minutes we had picked up two gannet heads, one of which had been singed in the fire. The limpness of both told of recent killing. Unlike Ethelred the Unready, one could always depend on Herb Grubner who now, true to form, produced from one of his pockets two white cotton specimen bags of the exact size we needed. One of these soon became bloodstained by its contents.

Whether these were the only two gannets taken it was impossible to say, though a survey of two sub-colonies nearest to the camp strongly suggested the number was greater, for here the tally of empty nests was about 30% instead of the 20% found elsewhere. In addition there were more "unemployed" adult birds than usual, which were in a shy and disturbed condition when we approached the sites.

We thought it very probable that the party had found fewer muttonbirds than expected, and so supplemented the catch from the neighbouring gannetries. Vic picked up half a loaf which had been left behind, and when he tested it for freshness his thumb sank into the bread. There was little more we could do for the present apart from noting details of the camp,

145

and completing our photographic coverage of the incident.

Upon returning to the colonies near the landing place, known as Ohauora "a" and "b", we photographed these for the record before making a start on banding. As will be recalled, our first visit had been mainly in the nature of a reconnaissance to determine what activities might be practicable for us to attempt. Our present venture was the next logical step, to extend our knowledge and secure practical training in banding gannets.

Although all of us had previous experience of this type of work, these birds were considerably larger than any we had tackled before, even the chick being provided with a powerful beak which it did not hesitate to use vigorously if given the chance. Wodzicki had very kindly presented us with a catcher. This consisted of two long light alloy tubes, one of which fitted fairly loosely inside the other. At one end a loop was formed by a length of rubber covered wire which was fastened to each piece of tubing. At the other end, the inner pipe protruded for about six inches, this section being covered with a hand grip. The noose could be closed by pulling back the handle, and opened again by returning the grip to its original position.

When using this tool it was a comparatively simple matter to drop the noose over the head of a chick, close it round the body and wings, and pluck it clear of a nest which might be six feet from the edge of the colony. It could then be held for another operator to band and record details before being returned to its original position. Other birds in the immediate neighbourhood showed not the slightest alarm, or even interest, though the youngster directly involved might have had reservations on the point.

Wodzicki had asked us to band as many birds as possible at the smaller "b" sub-colony, so Jack and Vic took charge there leaving Herb and I to work at "a". As we had only one catcher, the birds at "b" were lifted by hand. This was not as difficult as it sounds, since we were all provided with heavy gloves, and when approached the chicks would turn away from the operator, so enabling them to be secured without undue risk of pecking.

146

The bands were of monel metal, a light alloy, and in addition to a serial number on each there was a message asking the finder to return it to the Dominion Museum, Wellington. That year fitting was merely a matter of placing the band round the leg and closing the ends together with a pair of pliers. This type, however, was found to be unsatisfactory in service, since cases afterwards occurred where these were retrieved after having opened up and fallen off the birds. In subsequent years an improved band was used, incorporating a tongue at one end which had to be passed through a corresponding slot in the other side and bent over. This naturally made fitting a longer job, but on the other hand it would take a gannet version of Houdini to lose one of these.

While working, we were able to note the commensalism which had been reported by other observers. This has been defined as "the state of an animal living with or off another without being parasitical." This may seem to many to be a fine, or even artificial, distinction. In this case the red-billed gull mingled with the gannets, always on the look-out for an easy meal.

The adult gannets fished an area within a fifty mile radius of the island. This extensive working circle was necessary because of the very large number of birds to be fed at the peak of the breeding season, also the healthy appetites they enjoy. In Royal Navy slang a greedy person always used to be called a gannet. At White Island there were literally thousands of adult birds, plus chicks, the latter being able to consume their own weight in fish during the course of twenty-four hours.

On returning from a fishing expedition the parent would open its beak wide, whereupon the chick would thrust its bill inside. The older bird then regurgitated the food, which would be greedily swallowed by the young. On occasion an adult would for some reason disgorge away from its nest, and such an opportunity was seized by every gull within reach, whose pugnacity more than made up for the great disparity in size between the two species. One of our tasks was to note where possible the fish which had been caught, so we had to race the scavengers to the scene. One spew we examined consisted of eight garfish, herring and pilchard up to 25 cm. long.

The difference between a commensal and a parasite was brought home to us the following year, for we received a request from Wodzicki to collect any insects we might find while banding the birds. It appeared that Dr Theresa Clay, of the Department of Entomology at the British Museum, was undertaking a study of the parasites of New Zealand seabirds. One might think this a somewhat unlikely subject to select, since the essential field work lay on the other side of the world. She obviously had to have specimens, of which we were able to find only a few on the birds and nests. Later on, however, when Vic retrieved a dead gannet from the sea near his home, he struck a real bonanza in the parasite department. Apart from an advice that our haul contained no mallophaga, we heard nothing further of Dr Clay's researches.

One of the principal objects of our studies on the gannet was to determine whether populations of colonies were increasing or not. This was of particular importance at White Island, where there were grounds for thinking that numbers tended to fluctuate over a period to a greater extent than elsewhere in the country. While a census of the breeding areas was thus very desirable, it presented us with considerable difficulties, the usual state of affairs on the island.

The main trouble, of course, was lack of time, since there was an obvious limit to the amount of work which could be crammed into a single day. Although the Ohauora colonies were close to the landing at Bungalow Beach and could be reached easily, both Otaketake and Te Matawiwi took a good deal longer. Even when at the various locations, such vantage points as there were did not offer sufficiently comprehensive views to permit ease of counting.

Despite these limitations I was determined to make a start in this direction. Photographs of the various colonies taken over the period 1912–49 were available, and it would be a fairly simple matter when in the field to identify the spots from which these views had been obtained. It therefore seemed to be a constructive idea to prepare another set from the same points in 1959, which could then be compared with the earlier records to determine expansion or shrinkage in each nesting area.

Since the photographs could do little more than illustrate the extent of the areas occupied, we sought to add detail by adopting the random sampling technique. This consisted of selecting reasonably average sections of the colonies, where we counted the number of empty nests, those with chicks, and the remainder still containing eggs. In this way information was collected from which percentages could be calculated to give a fair indication of the overall position.

Cole had left us the dinghy, and when we finished work at Ohauora, Vic and Jack pushed off from the beach to row along the coast to have a look at the Te Matawiwi colonies. These were situated on the steep slopes of West Point, a commanding headland cut off from the former campsite by a series of deep gullies which, with the soft loose soil, made a land approach both slow and tiring. The best way to travel was by boat as far as the Te Hokowhitu stream bed, the last of the declivities, and then to climb through the pohutukawas to the crest of the bluff.

Herb and I set off in the opposite direction. We had little difficulty in finding the old track used by the workers when going from the camp to the factory, and as we followed it we gained height until really spectacular views of the mainland coast opened out before us. It crossed a number of gullies running down the cone, but since the path was high on the slopes these were usually not formidable. In one case, however, the original bridge spanning a larger than usual ravine had caved in. We tried to construct a makeshift crossing with what timber we were able to drag up to the track, but neither of us had much confidence in the result of our efforts. Rather than take the risk of an accident, we left the path and climbed higher until we were able to cross without further trouble.

As we neared our objective we struck southwards off the track

149

to pass through the scrub. This appeared to be quite dead, and as it was heavily laden with ash we collected an unwanted coating of dust by the time we emerged on the broad bare ridge which terminates abruptly at Gannet Point.

Our operations here took much the same form as at Ohauora, and we also made an unusual find. This was a muttonbird chick, covered with down, which was in the bright sunshine instead of sheltering below ground in the normal way. The poor creature seemed ill at ease as it crouched in the remains of a wind-eroded burrow, so we collected a few pieces of dead wood which were lying around and placed these over what was left of the hole to give the bird more protection.

When our work was completed we slithered down the steep loose surface into the ravine which separates the main colony from its smaller annexe on a lower shelf. Gilberd told me, with some amusement, that the 1914 enterprise built a jetty at the foot of this gully. It was certainly hard to see of what possible use it could have been in such an out of the way spot, and no trace of it remained in 1959.

Shortly afterwards we saw *Mako* cruising towards us, towing her dinghy, for she had picked up our colleagues at West Point to save them a long pull. Vic rowed ashore to collect us. I went on board, taking the packs and gear from Herb, who then made to follow me. At that moment the swell began to carry the boat clear of the shore; he hesitated, with his right foot in the dinghy and his left on a rock, looking for all the world like a dancer doing the splits. In another moment he would have collapsed into the sea, so I hastily grabbed his clothing and dragged him unceremoniously over the stern.

Mako took us on to Crater Bay, where we went ashore taking with us the telegraphist, who wanted to have a look round. Although on this occasion our sojourn was a fairly short one, we were able to note the changes from our previous visit, which are dealt with in a later chapter.

We re-embarked and headed for home after a long and tiring day. Cole had proved his mettle as an angler with a splendid kingfish, which he kindly presented to us. It provided a generous supply of delicious steaks for our families. In return, on our arrival at Ohope, Vic went on a hasty foraging expedition for milk. *Mako* had no refrigerator aboard, and fresh supplies were usually something of a problem.

Our findings on gannet poaching were duly reported to Douglas McKay, the resident wildlife ranger at Whakatane, and I heard no more of the matter for some months. One evening early in the following June, however, he came to see me, bringing with him Mr H.F. Hamlett, of the Department of Internal Affairs, Rotorua. They told me that charges had been laid against eleven Maoris who had been aboard the *Aio* when she was intercepted, and Hamlett wished to know if I was willing to appear in court as a witness for the Crown. At that time I was the local secretary of the Royal Forest and Bird Protection Society of New Zealand, and agreed to do what I could to help the Department in what promised to be a difficult case, since there was no more than inferential evidence to connect the accused with the poaching which had undoubtedly taken place.

Hamlett and McKay collected me on a fine winter morning, and we enjoyed a leisurely drive of forty miles or so to Opotiki, where we called upon an obliging local photographer. It was desired to offer colour slides in evidence, and we borrowed a viewer for the magistrate's use. Opotiki was then a quiet country town, for all its stirring past as a rebel stronghold and later military settlement, of which it seemed to be dreaming in the bright sunshine.

The little courtroom was quite full when we entered. I strolled across to the press table, and after introducing myself said:

"I suppose you'll be reporting this gannet poaching."

"Rather!" the lady representing the *Opotiki News* replied warmly. "It's not often we get an interesting case."

One could appreciate her point of view as we sat through the usual collection of motoring offences, few of which took up much of the court's time. When a defendant did put in an appearance, he was read a homily on the dangers of his ways while he stood there looking rather foolish. There was an odd case or two dealing with debt collection, but at last came the event we were waiting for, the Crown versus Sidney Allison, Ronald Brown, Charles Edwardson, Benjamin Gage, Duncan Moore, Roman Moore, George Newth, Tona Nuri, John Pirini, Leo Pirini and Peter Richard Warren.

According to one story I heard, the Maoris had been unable to find any local solicitor willing to take on the task of defending them. It seemed much more likely to me that as they had little faith in our chance of winning the case it would simply be an unnecessary expense to be legally represented. They were supported in this belief by well-informed opinion, since at the lunch adjournment the clerk of the court said quite frankly to my friends and me:

"My goodness, you people have a hard row to hoe."

It might seem at first sight that in appearing without a solicitor to defend them they were delivering themselves into our hands. In fact this was not so, for in the interests of justice Mr L.N. Ritchie, S.M., quite rightly set himself the object of seeing to it that the defendants' case did not suffer as a result of their ignorance of the law.

As principal witness for the Crown, I was called to open the case. In reply to Hamlett's questioning I related the events leading up to the attempted interception of the muttonbirders' launch. There was some confusion about the name *Aio*, which in capital letters on the bow of the boat suggested a fishing vessel with the registration number *A 10*. Having finally cleared this hurdle, I was asked to give an account of the gannet breeding cycle and colonies to make matters more intelligible to the court.

The hearing then passed on to the muttonbirders' camp at the time of our arrival. I described the finding of the two gannet heads. These grisly remains had spent the last few months in cold storage, and the prosecutor now caused a minor sensation in court by producing them for identification. The defendants' faces fell at the sight of their pigeons (or rather gannets) coming home to roost.

The prosecution wished to establish that the birds had been killed on the same morning as the heads were found. Since rigor mortis had not set in when we picked these up, and one was still bleeding, this was evidently the case. The point was also made that bread left nearby was still fresh at that time, although the weather was warm and dry. It had not laid there long enough to be eaten either by the red-billed gulls or the Maori rat, whose footprints were numerous in the mud of a stream bed adjoining the camp site. Cooking stones appeared to have been used recently.

The Crown case depended to an uncomfortable degree upon circumstantial evidence, which Hamlett was determined to make as complete as possible. To this end he brought out the point that we had originally intended to go to the island from the Ohiwa wharf on 18 November, but sea conditions were such as to make repeated crossings of the shoals at the harbour entrance an undesirable hazard. These bar-bound ports can be dangerous to even the most experienced of captains, as was the case with Stein's father, who commanded the s.s. *Aupouri*, and was drowned at Opotiki. By contrast, photographs of favourable sea conditions on the 22nd. were exhibited to the court, also others showing the meeting with the *Aio*.

Further evidence was produced to illustrate the high rate of occupancy of one of the colonies when photographed by McKay on 17 November as compared with a much lower density in our own pictures taken five days later. In reply to a question as to whether the birds might have flown off during the interim, I pointed out that this was impossible since they would not grow feathers for several more weeks.

Hamlett now concluded his questions, and Sidney Allison cross-examined me. He asked how recently I believed the hangi to have been used, but I replied that not having felt the warmth of the stones it was impossible for me to say whether or not these had been heated on the morning of the 22nd. I confirmed that one of the gannet heads was still warm when picked up.

I then stood down, and was replaced in the witness box by McKay. He had been at sea on the muttonbirding patrol in

H.M.N.Z.S. *Mako* from 15–21 November, and testified to rough weather during the period. Perhaps over-eager to stress the point, he went so far as to say that a landing at the island would have been impossible before the 21st.

This brought a dramatic intervention from the floor of the court. One of the defendants, I forget which, possibly with memories of film courtroom scenes in mind, sprang to his feet with arm outflung. Pointing to the witness he shouted:

"That man's a liar!"

The magistrate was pained by this interruption. He took the interjector quietly but firmly to task:

"I will not have that word used in this court. Don't you realise that you are accusing this man of perjury? You may say he is mistaken; you may not say he is a liar."

Duly chastened, the offender subsided into his seat. McKay was re-examined on the point, and his amended statement that a landing would certainly have been dangerous if not impossible was accepted without further demur.

One of the accused, Warren, was an honorary wildlife ranger appointed by the Department of Internal Affairs, his duties including the supervision of the way in which mutton-birds were hunted, also the preparation of returns showing the numbers taken. Hunters were legally required to remove the partly-grown chicks from the ground by means of a length of cane, to one end of which were attached pieces of wire with the ends pointing outwards. When the cane was rotated in the burrow, the points of the wire became entangled with the chick's fluffy down, so that it could be drawn out by pulling back the stick.

This was sometimes disregarded as being too slow a method, the hunter using a jungle knife to dig out the bird, damaging or destroying the burrow in the process. Wildlife officers have also expressed to me their doubts about the reliability of the tallies received from the various parties. They believe the figures may be too high, for if meagre returns were sent in the closure of hunting grounds might be accelerated.

Upon being called as a witness, Warren was cautioned by

the magistrate that he need not answer any question which might tend to incriminate him. According to his testimony, the whole party went ashore on the 21st. They found mutton-birds scarce as the island had been worked over by a previous party, but while there they did not see anyone else or any other boats. In the evening they had a hangi at the camp. He, with Christie (the master of the launch) and Nuri slept aboard the *Aio*. In reply to a question from the bench, Warren said the first time he had seen the gannet heads was in court.

The magistrate told the accused he was trying to help them as they had no counsel, and invited them either to give evidence or to address the court if they wished. Duncan Moore then said that they had been accused of killing gannets, but nobody had seen them on the island.

In his summing up Ritchie pointed out that McKay's list of the accused was, so far as the court was concerned, merely hearsay, and could not be accepted as evidence. Warren's testimony, however, had established that the whole party as named had been ashore on the island. After they left early on the morning of the 22nd. the gannet heads were found in fresh condition, so he must consider those who slept ashore as having participated in the poaching. He therefore convicted all except Nuri and Warren (Christie had not been named in the charge) and fined each £3 with £1.16s. 8d. costs. Since the maximum fine for the offence was £50, they had certainly got off lightly.

When McKay was interviewing the *Aio* party before the charges were laid, Newth had denied poaching gannets. On the other hand he volunteered the information that he had taken muttonbirds in an illegal manner. He was now charged with the offence, and fined £1 with £1.10s. 0d. costs. The honesty which he and Warren showed in acting against their own interests may well be contrasted with the dealings of some of the people connected with White Island Products.

After making due allowance for these being first offences, the fines inflicted were too low to act as a deterrent in the future. Stein told me at the time that gannet poaching in some areas of the Hauraki Gulf was so bad as to threaten the future existence of entire colonies. There is little point in having conservation legislation if its purpose is to be frustrated by the imposition of no more than token fines on the comparatively rare occasions when offenders are brought to book.

The *Aio* continued to make periodic visits to White Island for several years afterwards. When returning from a muttonbirding venture on 17 November 1967 the launch was overtaken by bad weather, and Christie ran for what shelter there was to be found in the lee of Whale Island, where the party spent the night.

Early the following morning, although conditions were not greatly improved, the *Aio* left for Opotiki. About 400 yards from the harbour entrance Warren, who was in the cabin, saw to his horror Christie, Allison and another man washed overboard by a big wave, leaving nobody at the helm. He rushed out to the tiller and brought the head of the launch round in an attempt to rescue his friends, but found the engine could not make headway against the heavy seas. With the boat drifting towards the shore Warren decided that as there was only sufficient fuel left for half an hour's running he had better try to enter the harbour, though he had little confidence in his chances of being able to do so in the circumstances.

He told the remaining eleven men to put on their lifejackets, and as the launch headed towards the river she lifted successfully to allow two large waves to pass beneath her. The third brought disaster, for the boat swung to one side and broached to, being overturned in the surf. Most of the occupants were thrown clear, but three men named Hayes, two brothers and a son, were trapped in the wreck. They managed to struggle clear, and eventually reached the shore with all their companions, including those originally washed overboard, a feat which was described as "nothing short of a miracle." Tragedy was not averted, however, for John Joseph Hayes of Taneatua was dead when brought on to the beach, leaving a widow and seven children to mourn his passing.

Peril on the sea is unfortunately only too common along this coast, which has a melancholy history of shipwrecks.

On 18 November 1961 my colleagues and I were due to be taken once again on a banding expedition to White Island by H.M.N.Z.S. *Mako*. Her commander had spoken to me on the telephone earlier in the week, when he put into Whakatane to land two of his crew, one to visit a dentist and the other a doctor.

On the afternoon of the 17th a friend of mine, Allan Pullar, drove a visitor from the D.S.I.R. to the car park at the mouth of the Whakatane River. They had been on a tour of inspection, and as they discussed its results they saw *Mako* approaching. The stranger, used to the spaciousness of the port at Wellington, said:

"Surely they will never bring that thing in here."

"Oh yes," replied Pullar airily, "we'll show you how it's done."

Never was there a more devastating example of famous last words. Allan told me later:

"We simply couldn't believe our eyes. As we sat there watching, the *Mako* came straight up on to the rocks below us!"

The vessel was bringing home the wildlife ranger from the muttonbird patrol. It appeared there had been some misunderstanding on lining up the shore leading marks to enter the river, with this disastrous result. The ship had grounded on a rock shelf, and her engines were unable to free her. Since the tide had begun to ebb, the passing minutes made it certain that she would have to stay where she was at least until the return of high water.

About 4 p.m. I had a phone call from Jack London to say that the launch was aground just inside the river mouth. In those days Vic Davis and I both worked at Whakatane Board Mills, so I went along to his office to tell him the bad news. We drove into town, and on approaching the harbour entrance the plight of the stranded vessel was only too obvious. The falling tide had left most of her forward half high and dry on the rocks, where she had settled with a pronounced list on her starboard bilge.

We left the car and walked down to the beach to meet a

young lieutenant wearing a worried frown, as well he might, while he surveyed his stricken ship. We introduced ourselves, and after a short conversation Vic proposed that we should give him what help we could pending the arrival of a salvage team from the naval dockyard at Auckland. Since this would have to travel more than two hundred miles by road, it obviously could not arrive until late that night, and much valuable time might be lost.

The captain, possibly still a serving officer, may be called Lieutenant X. He was grateful for any assistance which might be forthcoming, since no doubt a future court of enquiry was figuring largely in his thoughts at that moment. He could have had little conception then of what a warm-hearted small town could achieve in the way of co-operation when its enthusiasm was aroused.

Davis once said of an indefatigable friend:

"You have to have people like that, or nothing would ever get done."

How true that was of himself, for although many people worked with a will that night he was always the leading spirit. After a hasty meal we hitched a trailer on to his car and loaded it with every conceivable piece of equipment we might need, even including his dinghy. By contrast my own toolbox seemed to be a very modest contribution.

In our absence the captain decided, quite rightly, that the vessel must be lightened as far as possible. It would then float off the shelf with a minimum of delay when the tide rose. The first and most obvious need was to remove the anchor cables from the lockers in the bow. The members of the ship's company detailed to carry out this task did not exhibit any marked degree of enthusiasm, for flaking the large quantity of heavy chain across the slippery and uneven surface of the rocky foreshore was hard work by any standard. Under the supervision of the coxswain, addressed by his commander as "Mr Christian", the job was eventually finished.

Vic and Lieut X were soon busy in the bowels of the ship to find out how much water she had taken, so I climbed overboard and waded through the ebbing tide to try to check the extent of the damage to the hull. The launch had struck on the port side, and a careful examination soon revealed the hole in the outer skin. Although the penetration was not very large, there had been a fair amount of chafing. The inner skin had been holed only by a piece of rock hardly the size of a man's fist, which was still embedded in the timber. After reporting the position to Vic and his colleague, I returned suitably armed with a crowbar and levered the rock clear. When I presented this to the captain he looked at it, and commented with some feeling:

"I'll have this mounted on an inkstand."

As the tide fell, *Mako* had settled on to her starboard side. This was very fortunate, since as she heeled over the damaged port side was lifted clear of the rocks, so permitting easy access for repair work. The leak now being above the surface, a pump was started to clear the bilges and further lighten the ship, some two or three tons of water disappearing over the side.

Vic was the electrical engineer at Whakatane Board Mills, and able to arrange for his assistant, Ken Burt, to bring an emergency floodlighting plant from the works. This was set up on the foreshore, the lamps being directed to the damaged area on the ship's side. About this time I happened to glance shorewards, and was impressed by the sea of faces which showed the size of the gallery of onlookers we had attracted.

We now set to work on repairing the leak. To cover the small hole in the inner skin, a rubber mat from the wardroom was sacrificed, cut to size and tacked in place. Polyethylene sheeting was then secured over the much larger gap left in the outer hull after the worst of the ragged chafing had been stripped away, both of these patches being made as watertight as possible by liberally daubing a black bitumastic preparation round the edges. A good deal more became smeared over those handling it, with results which appeared comic to the rest of us if not to them. A further note of light relief came from a would-be helper wading out from the shore. He accidentally stepped in a hole in the submerged rocks, and promptly disappeared up to his neck in the black waters.

159

The Board Mills having provided a good deal of help, the subsidiary company, Whakatane Timber Mills, now joined in. The polyethylene patch obviously needed proper protection, and the necessary planking was soon forthcoming, Vic driving home plenty of long nails to secure this outer sheathing. Charlie Dickens, the sawmill manager, could not resist supplying the finishing touch by painting the legend, in large black letters on the radiata pine, "Board Mills Kauri."

The port side being as watertight as we could make it, a careful watch was kept on the level of the remaining water lying in the starboard bilges as the tide began to make once again, since it was possible that further damage might have been caused when the *Mako* heeled over. To our relief the rising tide produced no increased flooding inside the ship.

With the repair work now completed, attention turned to the problem of refloating *Mako*. This could evidently not be attempted until the early hours of the morning though, as a result of lightening, the ship's draught would be less than when she grounded, so we hoped she could be moved before the tide reached its peak.

The big question, of course, was how *Mako* would behave when (or if) we could get her free. It was believed the steering was damaged, and it was not known for certain whether the propulsion was still in working order, as a propeller blade had struck a rock earlier. The main risk was that when she floated clear the incoming tide might sweep the launch broadside on to the rocks, and so cause much worse damage than before.

An anchor had been laid out astern, but this was not thought sufficient to stand up to the probable strain. Arrangements were therefore made with a fisherman named Cooper for his launch *Roselyn* to lie astern of *Mako*. By hauling on a towrope when the time came, he could not only prevent her from broaching to but also help in refloating.

With *Roselyn* in position, the harbourmaster attempted to fire a rocket line to her. This was spectacular but unsuccessful, as it appeared that the apparatus was not accurate enough to drop the line on to such a small target. Someone therefore had to

The 1933 Crater Lake, golden with a film of sulphur

Jack London cautiously nears the edge of Noisy Nellie

Looking down into the crater of Noisy Nellie in 1958. It has since become a lakelet

Disphyma australe (mesembry themum) in flower

The gannet nestling, born naked, is soon clothed in a mass of snow-white down

do it the hard way by rowing out with the towrope in a dinghy.

There was bound to be a serious risk of *Mako* being holed again when she moved, in which event it would be desirable to have a large pump on board ready to keep her afloat. Several of the Whakatane Borough Council staff, Messrs Cuthbert, King, Pollard and two others, brought a new pump to the beach.

The really difficult part of the job was to get it aboard. It was lowered into a dinghy and moved out, there being perilously little freeboard under such gross overloading. The starboard deck of *Mako* was close to the water; it was not only tilted at a very steep angle but was also so slippery with a coating of fuel oil that it was hard to walk, much less to handle a heavy motor-driven pump. In the absence of any form of lifting tackle this had to be brought aboard by sheer manpower, but somehow we managed it. The equipment was new, and we stood by expectantly as it was started. Our faces quickly fell, for it seized up almost at once, and would obviously be of no use that night.

The only course was to try for a replacement, and while some of us started the weary business of returning the pump to the shore others set out to scour the town for another one. It was now late at night, and Lieut-Cdr L.G. Lawry, the officer in command of the Fisheries Protection Patrol, arrived from Auckland in charge of the dockyard salvage party. He was rowed out to *Mako* to supervise the refloating attempt.

A second launch made fast to *Mako* having, by a coincidence, the same name as the stranded vessel. About an hour before high water another pump arrived on the waterfront and was loaded into a dinghy. It was too late, however, for *Mako* no longer lay inert. Once again she showed signs of life as she began to bump gently up and down on her keel as the rising tide lifted her.

It was decided to make a first attempt at refloating, and after about ten minutes the ship slid clear of the rocks without further mishap. Because of the rudder damage the Whakatane *Mako* went ahead to tow the naval launch to the wharf.

161

The bright full moon was by now sinking low in the sky over Whale Island. Vic and I reloaded all the gear on his trailer, and he took me home on his way back to Ohope. How thankful I was to get to bed about 3 a.m. after an absence of more than twenty hours.

On the following day skindivers made a thorough examination of *Mako's* hull, and after repairs to the steering the launch sailed for Auckland at 3.15 p.m., the weather fortunately being excellent. When she was slipped at Devonport dockyard, our "Board Mills Kauri" patch was still firmly in place.

A letter written on behalf of the Commodore, Auckland (then absent on duty) which I received shortly afterwards included the passage:

"The assistance rendered by you and your party during the time H.M.N.Z.S. *Mako* was aground is very much appreciated."

Vic also had letters of thanks for his services both from the captain of *Mako* and his commanding officer. And that, I thought, was that.

A few weeks after this eventful night I left New Zealand on a somewhat leisurely journey round the world, and did not return until June, 1963. My daughter was by then a student at the Epsom Teachers' Training College, so the family settled in Auckland.

When shaving one sunny morning in August I heard my wife answer a knock at the front door, followed by a conversation which sounded as though the caller was Vic. Upon going into the lounge to greet him, I was rather staggered to be confronted by a complete stranger. Our visitor introduced himself as Graham D. Speight, then the Crown solicitor in Auckland, and subsequently a judge of the Supreme Court.

Although he was not Davis, the latter was none the less responsible for his unexpected appearance. When commenting on the efforts of our party in the salvage work, Vic had written:

"Their reward was in the satisfaction of seeing *Mako* refloated."

Speight now explained that Mr A.E. Cooper, owner of the fishing launch *Roselyn* which had assisted in freeing *Mako*

162

from her rocky bed two years before, required some more tangible recompense. This was understandable since while we had been amateur well-wishers, he earned his living from the sea. Towage could therefore be regarded as part of his normal employment.

The point at issue was that the Navy considered his bill to be excessive.

"We don't mind buying him another engine for his boat," said Speight, "but we do draw the line at paying for a new hull as well."

Cooper was now seeking judgment for his claim before Mr Justice Gresson in the Supreme Court, and the Crown was at a disadvantage since its case depended to some extent upon naval witnesses, whose evidence might not be thought entirely unbiassed.

Perhaps with this in mind, Speight had secured the attendance of William Waugh, the harbourmaster, and Kenneth Orchard of Whakatane as civilian witnesses for the defence. Orchard was a well-known yachtsman who also earned his living as a boatbuilder. While he was undoubtedly an expert on anything connected with the local waterfront, he had not taken part in the salvage work. In addition to this there was the point that if he gave evidence against the interests of a Whakatane fisherman, it might be prejudicial to his livelihood, which depended to some extent upon the goodwill of Cooper and his friends.

While feeling reluctant in these circumstances to summon Orchard as a witness, Speight believed it would be necessary to do so until his telephone rang one day. It was a long distance call from Ohope. Davis, who had noticed the newspaper report of the opening of the case, told Speight that I had just returned and supplied my address. The reason for the solicitor's breakfast-time visit was to find out if I would be willing to appear in place of Orchard. I naturally agreed at once so he arranged to collect me early in the afternoon.

In company with Lt-Cdr Lawry, who had flown all the way from Singapore for the hearing, he called for me after lunch.

Being in good time we stopped for a coffee on our way to court, during which my companions dismissed as pure rumour a story which had been current in Whakatane after the affair. This was to the effect that the dockyard party brought with them explosives to blow up the *Mako* if salvage attempts had failed. Not that this would have affected my testimony in any event, since even if true it would have been outside my personal knowledge and thus could not have been stated in evidence.

The hearing was then about to enter its fourth and final day. Counsel for the plaintiffs had stated that the court, acting in its Admiralty jurisdiction, was required under section 357 of the Shipping and Seamen Act of 1952 to determine a reasonable sum for salvage.

Adolphus Edward Cooper, owner of the *Roselyn*, said in evidence that he believed the *Mako* "could not have stood another tide" on account of the pounding she was taking from the heavy seas. "Apart from that, without the assistance of my boat to hold her in position she would have turned broadside on to the breakers that were rolling in across the bar." He was offered £160 for his services by the Navy, but considered this insufficient.

After taking legal advice, he and those who acted as his crew on the night of 17–18 November, David Anderson, Edward Ray Cooper and Neil Alexander Larsen, brought this action against the Attorney-General in respect of the Navy Department, claiming an award of £2,500. I could well appreciate how embarrassing it would have been for Orchard to have appeared, since I had been on friendly terms with two of the plaintiffs for some years.

In his opening address for the defence Speight did not accept Cooper's version of events:

> "The attitude of everybody concerned in the refloating at Whakatane was enormously helpful. But although we were glad enough of Mr Cooper's assistance, without being dishonourable about it, we say it was not necessarily crucial, although it was undoubtedly a factor, in getting *Mako* off."

Upon entering the witness box I was confronted by the defence counsel now suitably disguised in wig and gown, who asked me to describe events on the night in question. It was quite a long recital, or it seemed so to me, given to the accompaniment of furious hammering on a typewriter by a typist invisible in a frosted glass cubicle as a transcript of the evidence was prepared. Every so often there would come a pause whilst the paper was ripped out of the machine, to be handed to a policeman who distributed the copies.

When I at last reached the refloating of the *Mako*, I was asked to go to a large chart of Whakatane Harbour and to mark the spot where I believed *Roselyn* was lying at the time. To my irreverent mind it was strongly reminiscent of the party blindfold game of pinning the tail on the donkey. From the variety of positions already indicated, the results looked just about as accurate. The plaintiffs' crosses were prominent outside the harbour altogether, in situations which would have required a very long towrope indeed to have linked the two vessels. As my pencil hovered over the paper both counsel were not far from the back of my neck, but I planted my mark boldly and returned to the witness box.

Mr Chilwell (now QC) began his cross-examination with a series of comparatively innocuous questions, as Hamlett had done in his famous duel with Peter Warren. I rather expected him to do his best to upset my testimony about the weather, as this was certainly important to his case. It became apparent he was moving in this direction when he suddenly asked my opinion as to the reliability of the staff member at Whakatane Board Mills who, as one of his duties, recorded climatic details every day.

I affirmed my confidence in his reports.

"Then would it surprise you to know that on the morning of the 17th he stated the sea was choppy?"

"That may well have been so at nine o'clock in the morning. It was not so at five in the evening," I replied.

Counsel was about to proceed when Gresson interposed:

"Mr Chilwell, I can see that you are trying to shake the

witness's testimony, but he has given his evidence and I don't think Marshall Hall could change it."

Probably disgusted by my stubbornness, counsel desisted from further questioning and I stepped down. After further witnesses had been called for the defence, the hearing closed and those who had been engaged on the Crown side adjourned to a convenient hotel to fight the Navy's case all over again in retrospect.

In his subsequent judgment Gresson said the *Roselyn* made a modest but worthwhile contribution to the saving of the *Mako*, which might not have been refloated so soon without the *Roselyn's* assistance.

"The *Mako*, nevertheless, was not in a situation of extreme danger; I think the probability is that she would have floated off at the next high tide in any event — though with that delay she would necessarily have suffered some slight additional damage."

There was at no stage any appreciable danger to life, and the sea and weather conditions were moderate, in his view relatively favourable. He awarded the plaintiffs the sum of £725.

In a subsequent letter Speight commented:

"You will have seen the result in the paper, which we regard as not unsatisfactory."

The Navy provided transport to White Island on several further occasions, but apart from one abortive departure from Auckland, which got no farther than North Head at the harbour entrance, I did not participate.

VIII

Vulcan's Furnace

The word "volcano" is derived from Vulcan, the Roman god of fire and patron of workers in metals, known also in Greek mythology as Hephaestus. He was credited with building forges on earth, and was so industrious that these still remain throughout the world as the volcanoes of today. Evidently even the great pioneers of Western thought were but little in advance of the Maori in seeking to explain features of the landscape which they did not understand.

Despite the island's legendary association with fire, there has been a reluctance on the part of scientific opinion in recent years, in view of the present stage of the decline in activity (or old age) of the volcano, to accept the possibility of flames being seen. In Marsden's case this is no doubt well-founded, since he was looking at the peak from a distance of more than fifty miles, and save in the event of an exceptional outburst such as the Tarawera eruption it is very unlikely that anyone could detect live flame in the daytime when so far away.

But what of some of the later reports? Polack wrote:

"This island is in continual ignition. At dusk, the flames issuing from the crater, situated in the centrical part of the mountain, are distinctly visible for some miles; and long after the mariner has lost sight of the island from the horizon, the ascending smoke of this natural furnace suffices to point out its locality. I was at one time becalmed off this island for six days, during which period the crater emitted a vast volume of black smoke during the day, and at night the flames were glaring."

He was also describing conditions of long ago, but in the year before the Tarawera eruption a correspondent of the

167

New Zealand Herald who visited the volcano reported a "solid column of flame . . . no flickering uncertain flame but a veritable pillar of fire" estimated to be over 800 feet high.

In May 1909 the second officer of the s.s. *Kaipara* recorded a "continuous volume of black smoke, in which flames were distinctly seen" between 2 a.m. and daylight. Since the ship was many miles from the island at the time, the activity must obviously have been considerable for it to be easily visible.

Within the last few years no more than small blue flames of burning sulphur have been noted. Red coloured steam or smoke could possibly be mistaken for flames in daylight, but at night any light could come only from fire. It seems that despite the falling off in its energies, the volcano could live up to its reputation at least until the early part of this century.

White Island's behaviour can be at once both fascinating and frustrating. Its thermal activity ensures constant if slow change in the appearance of the crater. If seen at intervals of a year or two this provides an unfailing source of interest when noting what has happened since the previous visit. On the other hand, no matter how I may try to describe recent conditions, these are almost certain to have changed by the time this book is completed.

Although the advent of the helicopter has greatly facilitated close inspection of volcanic peaks without the drudgery for the scientist of having to scale perhaps thousands of feet of steep ash or snow covered slopes, and indeed can lower him to the very lip of the cone if necessary, Whakaari may also be reached by sea. This has the important advantage of permitting a party with stores and whatever equipment may be needed to be landed in the actual crater at low cost.

There is the further point that while in the case of a comparatively young volcano the activity may be more violent, it is at the same time unlikely to be so varied in its nature and readily admissible to study as here. This is important, since the mounting of any expedition requires months of careful thought and planning. The actual time spent in the field may well be the briefest stage of the whole venture, for upon returning the various specialists in the party face a further long period of work evaluating and reporting their discoveries.

Scientists, like everyone else, need to relax a little at times, and are not always entirely serious when finding names for features of the crater. There was, for example, the case of a fumarole close to the western wall of the 1933 Crater. The surrounding rock glowed red hot at night like a coke fire, reaching temperatures of 850° to 900°C.

During 1967 Professor Robert H. Clark and his party from the Victoria University of Wellington were so impressed by this striking colour that they christened the vent Rudolf after the red-nosed reindeer of the comic song.

As if to demonstrate its resentment at such cavalier treatment, Rudolf grew in size during the year to a diameter of about twenty feet, and periodically threw up clouds of ash and gas, the latter being detected more than ten miles down wind from the volcano. It was discharged from the vent at speeds of up to 300 miles an hour, the ear-splitting roar from which could be clearly heard at Te Awapuia at the other end of the crater.

A century earlier Davy's map had aroused interest, but it showed little more than outlines of the coast, crater, two lakes and a pond. All three of the latter were boiling at the time he made the survey.

Two years later Dr Hector (later to become Sir James Hector, president of the New Zealand Institute) heard, probably from Dr Rolston, the surgeon of H.M.S. *Brisk*, that the warship was to make a call at White Island. He lost no time in urging Rolston and Lieut R.A. Edwin, R.N., to collect all the information they could while there with the object of preparing a scientific paper on their return.

They did so, and Hector, as secretary of the infant Auckland Institute, presented their account to a meeting held on 4 May 1868, at which bottled samples of material collected from the crater were on display. Edwin prepared a much more detailed map of the crater than Davy's. He also made a sketch of the area which, although not entirely accurate, gave a better idea of its appearance than could be gathered from the map alone.

169

The two lakes of 1866 had merged into a single sheet of water more than fifteen acres in extent. It had a uniform depth of about twelve feet, and the surface was fifteen feet above sea level. The temperature was now only 110°F., the fall from boiling point no doubt being due to the considerable increase in the volume of water. This feature was given the name Lake Hope. Although Captain Charles W. Hope had commanded H.M.S. *Brisk* during the seaborne attack on nearby Opotiki in 1865, it seems the choice was made in honour of Lieut Hope who, aboard a raft, took soundings in the lake for Rolston and Edwin.

One find in 1868 was a mud pool, or volcano, some twelve feet across with a temperature of 200°F., at the north-east end of the lake. This was of interest as an example of a type of activity which, though common enough to early observers, was much less so during my visits, when the usual form of vent was either a sulphur-depositing fumarole or steam jet. The intervening drainage of the lake and raising of the level of the crater floor by the 1914 lahar could, of course, have been largely responsible for this decline of mud pools.

The first serious scientific study of the volcano, as opposed to the necessarily cursory inspections of earlier visitors, was carried out by Dr L.I. Grange of the New Zealand Geological Survey. In April, 1927 he made an investigation of the sulphur and gypsum deposits, also of the gases from the fumaroles and waters of the hot springs. He prepared an excellent map of the crater, and followed up his initial studies in January, 1928, when he was joined by Dr Coleridge Farr from Otago and in April, 1929.

He made quite an impression upon Gilberd, who was himself no sluggard:

"Grange was one of the hardest workers I ever met. He had a standing arrangement with the cook for an early breakfast, for he liked to reach the crater rim by the time the sun came over the horizon. He would work in the crater all day, and never returned until dark."

There was then a unique formation aptly called Lot's Wife, a natural statue which at once evoked memories of the Biblical story. It has, alas, like so many other one-time attractions, long since been lost in the inescapable process of volcanic change. This has also claimed both Big Donald and Schubert's Fairy, two of the other outstanding features that Grange knew.

He found the gases to consist mainly of carbon dioxide, though sulphur dioxide and methane were also present. The water from the hot springs was fairly rich in hydrochloric acid, and contained a number of dissolved mineral salts.

Mention has already been made of the vagaries of the crater lake, which recorded its highest known point of 25 to 30 feet above sea level at the time of Hector's call in April, 1869. He reported "occasional outbursts of boiling water. . . rising to a height of several hundred feet." In the following year it completely disappeared, though returning shortly afterwards. This alternating behaviour continued until the dry period between 1886 and 1893, following which it was resumed until in 1909 Professor James Park estimated its area to be 40 acres.

After the drainage of the lake in 1914 various blowholes and minor craters became flooded from time to time, though the water area never again approached its earlier extent. The largest expanse in recent times may have been in 1960, when our party found shallow pools both in the 1933 Crater and an adjoining depression.

Once again the water had disappeared entirely by the following year. The bed of the 1933 Crater was then criss-crossed by large cracks. Vic went down for a closer look, and mentioned that he heard a gurgling noise coming from below the surface.

It is not clear why or how such a large blowhole as Noisy Nellie, formerly completely dry, should fill with water as it did during the sixties. In view of its size the volume would be considerable, even though it had grown shallower and wider, no doubt as the result of landslides. The supply would have to be mainly of subterranean origin, since the rainwater catchment in the immediate vicinity would be quite insufficient.

171

The high temperature of the water would also ensure a continous and appreciable loss from evaporation.

There can be little doubt that for some reason, possibly as a result of earth tremors, part of the widespread sub-surface water noted by Goosman has been diverted to the pit of Noisy Nellie. There may have been some increase in underground supplies, since it was not until 1967 that hot springs were seen on the beach at Te Awapuia. With such constant changes in the crater floor it is really impossible to decide whether there is more water or if it has merely been diverted to some new area.

The swelling of the crater floor noted by Kennedy and the subsidence reported by Goosman were not unique; such movements have since been carefully observed.

In 1951 James Healy, the volcanologist of Rotorua, sited marker pegs at various points to help in the preparation of an excellent map of the island which was published in 1959. When later on some of these were buried by new ash showers, he put in replacements. His compass bearings then showed discrepancies, from which he supposed there were magnetic disturbances in the southern area of the crater.

While these pegs were also intended to make it easier to map the changing face of the crater in the future, the method was extended by Clark's party in 1967 to study the waxing and waning of the floor. They added a further series, and by surveying levels at intervals the extent of any changes could be measured.

It was found that a build-up of pressure resulted in bulging of the surface. When this was relieved by an eruption of ash and gas there was a collapse, as might be expected. In the swelling phase some very high temperatures were recorded, from which it was inferred that the stem of molten rock in the throat of the volcano was very close to ground level.

The surface itself can also vary to a surprising degree. After the hot mud and brilliant colour display of 1958, Vic and I hoped for further attractive photographs the following year. We were to be sadly disappointed, the floor then having a brown coating, and while this showed up our footprints it was as firm as a hard tennis court. Almost all of the mineral salts had been buried by this new ash fall.

In 1960 mud was once again taking over, with a partial restoration of colour. Something completely new occurred in 1966, when a fine white ash like fresh cement covered a large area.

As in Goosman's case, Healy was actually present at the time of an eruption. It came from the Gilliver Crater on 19 November 1966, and was remarkable inasmuch as it took place in complete silence. More than this, instead of the ash and steam rising at once in the usual vertical column, it was initially discharged in a horizontal cloud, something not previously seen at the volcano. The crater was named in memory of Mr R.W. Gilliver, formerly of the Marine Department, who observed and photographed White Island for many years in the course of his duties.

Healy believes the 1914 rock slide was the result of chemical decomposition of the material underlying a section of the cliff extending back to a prominent fault line behind the crater rim. This can be clearly seen from the air, there having been a noticeable slumping of the area above the crack.

The fault now passes behind the highest peak on the island, Mt Gisborne. There is a good deal of geothermal activity at its foot, and at times even from the crest of the mountain. It is thus evident that conditions here are similar to those at the adjoining area in 1914.

It is at least likely that the highest part of the wall will one day collapse. Life should be quite exciting for anyone who happened to be visiting the crater flat at the time.

IX

Struggle for Existence

"The plant formations of White Island are of interest, as they exist under conditions scarcely paralleled elsewhere in the New Zealand region, namely in the presence of fumes of hydrochloric acid."

So wrote Dr W.R.B. Oliver in 1912 after his return from a most productive call at the island, for his was the first really scientific investigation of its fauna and flora. Prior to that time the volcanic phenomena of the crater had absorbed the attention of observers to such a degree that where any reference was made to botanical or zoological conditions it was generally hurried and often inaccurate.

When William Williams was acting as guide to D'Urville at the Bay of Islands he mentioned that during the missionaries' call at White Island in 1826 "they noted a few trees, but the rest is bare." He appears to have been speaking of the southern benches. Writing of the same occasion Gilbert Mair, senior, recorded "the north part is covered with a small scrub." He seems to have been the only one of the early visitors to confirm the existence of vegetation on the northern slopes.

Only twelve years later Polack, apparently referring to Te Matawiwi, claimed it to be "well covered with verdure." Rolston and Edwin, whose work in the crater in 1868 was quite thorough, were cursory in this respect:

"The vegetation seen (which could not be got at) was a dense scrubby green bush, growing all over the western end of the island. A grass was also observed on an inaccessible rock on the south bank, short and very green."

The rock would seem to have been either Gannet Point or

175

West Point, and while neither is particularly easy to reach these could not really be thought inaccessible. It also appears that the very green plant was not a grass at all, but in fact mesembryanthemum.

It is possible they were short of time when observing this area, but they did not mention the possibility of going ashore at Ohauora, which occurred to Hector, who landed for a brief period at Crater Bay two years later:

> "The least precipitous part of this slope (West Point) is covered with a dense vegetation of a dark green colour, probably ngaio scrub (*Myoporum laetum*). There is only one beach on this side of the island where it might be possible to land in very calm weather for the purpose of examining this vegetation, which appears to be quite inaccessible from the usual landing place."

Even so noted a botanist as Hector came to grief in his guess as to the identity of the plant cover, since ngaio is in reality a species unknown on the island.

Today a broad belt of forest and scrub clothes most of the south coast, while there are also quite sizeable areas on the northern benches. The dominant feature of the vegetation is a stand consisting almost entirely of pohutukawa (*Metrosideros excelsa*), and it seems fairly obvious that this has expanded to quite a considerable extent since 1826. Exactly a century later it was claimed to be "at least 100 acres" and, though White Island Products was seldom guilty of undue conservatism in its estimates, only usable timber was being considered in this context, so the shrubland was doubtless excluded. Forty years later a figure of 200 acres was given. Even the most casual glance at the southern side of the island now would surely suggest considerably more than "a few trees."

On our first visit we were surprised to note the youth of the pohutukawas, whose slenderness contrasted sharply with the gnarled giants which do so much to grace the bays and beaches of the Bay of Plenty. These fine old trees appear to delight in showing how they can thrive in adverse conditions, for often

A large rock carried half a mile by the lahar following the 1914 landslip

Te Awapuia (Crater Bay). Diomede Rock in the foreground. The factory ruins lie at the foot of Troup Head, with the Pinnacles in the background

Missing rails and scattered sleepers trace the route of the tramway from the quarry in 1972

a huge specimen clings to the near vertical face of a cliff so that one would think it impossible for the roots to gain a sufficient hold to sustain its great weight.

Raymond Buttle believed the present forest to be as much as two hundred years old, but did not mention how he arrived at this conclusion. Except in the case of a comparatively small minority of the trees this is most probably an over-estimate. The count of annual rings made upon a specimen 35 feet high which was felled by the 1949 expedition gave the age as 70 years, and Williams's reference to the scarcity of vegetation tends to bear out the likelihood that much of the forest has become established since he saw it.

There is, however, evidence to suggest that the present forest was not the first to grow upon the southern flanks of the volcano. When Dr Charles A. Fleming accompanied the 1947 expedition, he investigated a bank, consisting of sand and pebbles and standing about fifteen feet high, at the head of the boulder beach at Ohauora. He believed this to be part of the former sea bed, either deposited during the last Interglacial Age when the sea was at a higher level than today, or thrust up by a movement of the earth's crust.

In this formation he found fossils which, though poorly preserved, were considered to be those of pohutukawa leaves, fern root and flower stems of flax, plants whose present day counterparts still live on the island. In a subsequent paper contributed to the *New Zealand Journal of Geology and Geophysics* he suggested the possibility of fossilised wood being found in the future, from which carbon dating might reveal the age of these remains.

One of the many mysteries of the island is what happened to the forest between the fossil period and the present. So far as can be determined, volcanic activity has not been on a scale sufficient to bury trees, and the only alternative would seem to be destruction by fire. There was some evidence of this when several charred pohutukawa stumps were found at a height of 600 to 700 feet at the western end of the island by Dr W.M. Hamilton when he surveyed the area during 1949.

While the high rainfall of more than 60 inches (1,525 mm.) a year at once promotes growth of vegetation and reduces the fire hazard, it is obvious that the latter is an ever-present threat. As in all forests, dead leaves and other inflammable trash accumulate beneath the canopy. A simple combination of unfavourable circumstances, such as a shower of red-hot stones thrown up during an eruption and falling among the trees when the weather was dry, could easily start a blaze. In addition the island has been visited, perhaps for centuries, by fishermen and sulphur collectors, so that neglected camp fires cannot be ruled out as a possible cause of forest destruction.

Not only is the forest at risk by fire, for the emission of acid fumes and non-inflammable ejecta from the crater also have their effect. Oliver first pointed out in 1915 that if a north or north-east wind was blowing in wet weather, a fairly common event, the rain absorbed fumes during its fall and plant life was therefore showered with dilute hydrochloric acid, as a result of which he recorded burning at the edge of leaves. He went on to comment:

"Dead branches and twigs attached to the living plants are a conspicuous feature, and dead trees still standing are occasionally met with. It is evident that the plants have a hard struggle for existence, and possibly the fumes in the atmosphere act as preservatives, inhibiting the decomposition of the dead parts."

His observations on acid burns were amply borne out by Gilberd when he mentioned that the attempted cultivation of much-needed green vegetables had to be abandoned for this reason. He was also evidently correct in his theory that acid fumes had the property of preserving timber, numerous instances having been confirmed by later observers.

On our first visit to the southern benches in 1958 we noticed the tendency of dead branches and leaves to remain on the trees, as Oliver had indicated, and even the upper foliage was less dense than might have been expected. The following year we were oppressed by the feeling of working in a dead forest, for neither pohutukawa nor taupata (*Coprosma repens*) showed the slightest sign of life.

It would appear that fumes were primarily responsible for this extreme condition, but since the trees and shrubs were heavily laden with ash, which Goosman had found on analysis to be sulphur-bearing, it may be that the chemicals in this deposit were also partly to blame for the damage.

By 1960 we were amazed to note the extent of the recovery, particularly by the pohutukawa, which was not only showing a good growth of new leaf but even occasional flowers, although there was still some trace of the earlier defoliation.

One further hazard which has not previously been recorded was observed by Davis during a visit in 1968. Early in April of that year a tropical cyclone made its way southwards, giving rise to a storm of quite exceptional violence. This caused considerable property damage down the eastern side of the North Island, and wrecked the interisland ferry *Wahine* at the harbour entrance as the ship was approaching Wellington.

Vic was much impressed by the extent of the wind damage to the forest on the southern benches. Trees on the lower slopes of the cone were blown over, though those around the former campsite near the coast had not been affected. One peculiar feature was that the fallen trees did not face in one direction away from the eye of the wind as might have been expected, but were jumbled together in a confused manner.

One can only assume that the northerly gale, blowing over and round the peak, struck the forest from a variety of angles to produce this result. The loss of pohutukawas from this cause is certainly exceptional, but it has to be remembered that although these enjoy the benefit of what shelter there is from the north and east, the vegetation is still vulnerable on account of its exposed situation.

Setbacks such as this must inevitably retard development of plant life, but it would appear that the advance of vegetation, slow though it may be when compared with the luxuriant growth on the nearby mainland, is still well ahead of coverage

179

on the desolate upper slopes of White Island's closely related peak, Mt Tarawera.

When I walked over this desert-like expanse, more than seventy years after the great eruption, the ash and scoria surface was very similar to some areas of White Island. In some of the more sheltered places, such as gullies on the southern side of the mountain, there was a fair amount of weed growth. Trees, however, were represented only by *Pinus radiata*, specimens of which struggled to establish themselves. Each of these was rooted in pure scoria, the spindly trunk being surrounded with a thin layer of dead needles shed by the plant itself.

These pines were evidently the result of wind-blown seed, and were very stunted by comparison with parent trees in the large exotic forests of the Rotorua-Taupo district, which in favourable circumstances can grow as much as eight feet in a single year. On the lower areas of the mountain manuka (*Leptospermum ericoides*) had taken a firm hold, and it is rather remarkable that this ubiquitous member of our flora has failed to colonise suitable sites on White Island.

The southern forested sections of the island at least enjoy a far better soil than the very scanty covering of Tarawera. Although not particularly deep, it is considerably enriched by leaf mould, the sulphur content from ash showers, and excreta from the burrowing muttonbirds. As previously noted, the gannets nest up to and under the fringes of the trees, while occasional fallen trunks suggest that the breeding areas may have claimed part of the former forest. Whether the strength of the ammonia contained in gannet droppings is sufficient to have any deleterious effect on pohutukawas is unknown. It is possible that long contact with this chemical, allied to the puddling effect on the surface from constant movement of the birds, may eventually kill trees.

The vegetation has had, since the sheep disappeared, the further advantage of complete freedom from browsing animals. As a result of this both Dr W.M. Hamilton in 1947 and 1949, and the 1964 expedition under Robertson (son of the Rev F.H. Robertson, who visited the island for the gannet census in 1947) reported pohutukawa seedlings ranging from one to six inches high as being plentiful throughout the southern area. By contrast, on Whale Island before the clearance of goats, it was impossible to find a young plant which these animals had overlooked. One interesting point is that Hamilton found seedlings only in the shrubland, whereas Mr C.W. Sampson noted these in the actual forest area. Reports show a marked decline in the occupancy of muttonbird burrows during the intervening years, and the consequent reduced disturbance of the soil might have helped plants to become established.

Trees at the western end of the forest at Te Matawiwi are notably larger and healthier than those to the east at Otaketake. These are also growing more rapidly, as may be seen from the heights recorded in the following surveys:

Year	Otaketake	Ohauora	Te Matawiwi
1912	10–13 ft.	—	20–26 ft.
1949	—	—	30–45 ft.
1964	10–25 ft.	20–40 ft.	30–50 ft.

I have on two occasions grown pohutukawas from small seedlings. It was noticeable, as in other instances with native, flora, that with increasing size came an acceleration in the rate of growth. It may therefore follow that the forest took a proportionately longer time to reach the stature noted by Oliver in 1912 than to attain the greater canopy height seen by Sampson 52 years later.

A quite remarkable feature of the forest is found at its northern verge west of Otaketake, where Hamilton reported:

> "As the forest approaches its upper limit the canopy usually decreases slightly in height and then ceases abruptly, the foliage descending to the ground like a clipped hedge. Trees on the edge of the forest showed a new season's growth of 6–10 in., while shrubs a few feet away showed a growth of 0–2 in. only, with the tips of many of the older leaves killed back to half their length."

It is difficult to understand why the change should be so

181

sharply delineated, and one can only suppose that the configuration of the cone is such that fume-laden winds are more common and severe in their effects over the area above the forest proper, where the pohutukawas do not develop beyond the size of bushes. This theory is supported by the fact that trees are healthiest at the western end of the island which is kept largely free of fumes by the prevailing wind. The change becomes more marked from east to west, with the shrubland at a minimum above Te Matawiwi.

In the course of a climb to the low point on the south-west crater rim, I was able to see the way in which the plant grew at the upper limits of this scrub. Here it hugged the ground, the stems growing in a notably crooked and crabwise fashion with comparatively few leaves. This was quite foreign to its behaviour under normal conditions, when the multiple trunks of the young pohutukawa are at least reasonably straight, and while not reaching for the sky in the ramrod manner of the kauri or kohekohe, resemble other trees in their upright or leaning postures.

If the distribution of the southern forest has its peculiarities, its counterpart on the northern flank of the volcano is even more puzzling. It is very sparse along the coastline from Shark Bay to North-east Point, as might be expected since the westerly wind passing over the crater brings acid fumes in greater concentrations than elsewhere outside the cone. On the other hand, odd, patches of pohutukawa and taupata are found scattered about the broad benches and at the foot of the North Barranco, or gully, without apparent reason. Soil acidity or deficiencies, and perhaps thermal activity, probably play some part in causing this seemingly haphazard siting. Bird populations, with their attendant fertilising effect, are very much lower here than on the south coast. Storms approaching from the usual directions of north or east bring gales which undoubtedly subject vegetation to severe salt spray. The true explanation for the erratic growth of the trees may well lie in some combination of these adverse factors which is not yet, and may never be, understood.

The stand of pohutukawa is so dominant as to largely eclipse other forms of vegetation. Of the other two fossil forms found by Fleming, the better known is the native flax (*Phormium tenax*). This plant is very hardy, and no doubt well able to withstand the unfavourable conditions on the island. A botanist friend told me of a clump of flax, intended for planting on the mainland, which was inadvertently overlooked and left lying on the surface of the ground throughout the winter frosts, often quite severe in that district. When finally replanted in the spring, the long-suffering specimen grew as strongly as ever.

Perhaps because of this exceptional vitality it has been suggested that the plant was accidentally introduced to White Island by Maoris going there for fishing or other purposes. Kits, which are made of green flax, served the double purpose of bringing in food for the hunters and carrying away the birds or fish for which they had come. The material in damaged or mislaid baskets could easily have put down roots and thrived in the heavy rains.

So far as the plants in the forest are concerned, this may well have been the case. On the other hand, flax is more common in the shrubland on the slopes of Mt Ngatoro and on North-east Point, neither of which sites is suitable for camping. It is therefore possible that these colonies could have resulted from the seed produced in quantity along the mainland coast, or from plants originally established on the southern benches.

It is evident that here, as at Tarawera, the ash and scoria of recent volcanic activity, coupled with the lack of shade away from the trees, make little appeal to the large fern family which generally finds New Zealand conditions so much to its taste. The only member of this group is *Histiopteris incisa*, which is thought to have supplied the rhizomes found in fossil state. It is practically confined to the forest, often in association with flax. The foliage in this case also has been noted as sensitive to burning by the acid fumes.

Apart from the pohutukawa the most striking species is undoubtedly the one variously known as *Disphyma australe*, mesembryanthemum or ice plant. It grows best on the fringes of the gannetries, obviously taking advantage of the constantly

183

replenished supplies of guano. It has also joined flax in colonising to some extent the shrubland on Mt Ngatoro. The brilliant colour and lawn-like appearance of mesembryanthe-mum when seen from the sea more than a century ago led Rolston and Edwin to mistake it for grass. It can at least claim the unique distinction of having been found on the crater flat, in the vicinity of the old factory buildings.

The only grass on the island is in fact *Poa anceps*, which shares the ice plant's fondness for the verges of gannetries, though growing also in the lighter sections of the forest near Te Hokowhitu. It is, however, of a coarse tussocky nature, slippery underfoot when dry, and one can readily understand why such fastidious grazing animals as sheep would find it anything but appetising. Sladden was under the impression that bales of hay were brought from the mainland to feed them, but according to Gilberd this was not so, the unfortunate sheep being expected to live off the country, grass or no grass.

Sladden went on to suggest that such imported hay could also have brought weeds, and these are found, though to a far less extent than, for example, the severe infestation of thistle (*Onopordon acanthium*) which occurred on Whale Island some years ago. The sow thistle (*Sonchus oleraceus*) grows on White Island. Captain Cook was not alone in recognising its value as a green vegetable, for as puha it figured on Maori menus at least until very recently. It follows that in this case too the food kit may have been the agency by which it reached the volcano. A few other weeds such as fat-hen (*Chenopodium allanii*) and inkweed (*Phytolacca octandra*) also occur.

The native taupata (*Coprosma repens*), often used for hedging on the mainland, is another plant which prefers to grow near the gannetries. It is seldom seen with the usual mirror-like leaves, being sometimes hardly recognisable in an almost de-foliated state. This woebegone appearance strongly suggests that it exists here by sufferance rather than choice.

Plant species on the island are very restricted, less than a score being found at any one time. Those present in only small numbers, often weeds, have a tendency to disappear, which is unhappily only too contrary to normal experience. It seems unlikely that vegetation will make any great advance except perhaps in the long term when there has been a further substantial decline in both volcanic activity and resultant soil acidity.

X

"*The Meek Shall Inherit . . .*"

There is a fairly widespread sentimental belief that birds are as free as the air in which they fly. The lives of many species are in fact regimented by a routine almost as unbending as that which rules the lives of most of us.

An excellent example is provided by the gannet, which already had a well-established breeding colony on the Bird Rocks in the Gulf of St Lawrence when Jacques Cartier first explored eastern Canada in 1534. The White Island gannetries may be as old as this, and for the first account of these we are indebted to another sailor, Captain John Fairchild, who for some years commanded the Government coastal steamers *Hinemoa* and *Tutanekai*:

> "The habits of the gannet are so very strange that it may interest you if I give the results of my own experience with these birds. . . They commence laying about the 18th September, and it takes about thirty-three days to hatch out the young. The female lays two eggs; she keeps one and the male bird takes charge of the other, and each one hatches its own and afterwards looks after the wants of the young one. About the first of February the same thing is repeated. The second hatching takes place about the first week in March."

So Fairchild reported to Sir Walter Buller when the latter was writing his monumental *History of the Birds of New Zealand*. He continued:

> "I hardly think that there can possibly be a mistake in this, as I have carefully watched the habits of these birds during the last twenty years, whenever an opportunity offered."

187

In the field of famous last words these were fully the equal of Pullar's on the approach of the *Mako*, for not one of his statements was correct. The Captain undoubtedly rendered excellent service to the colony by tending the lighthouses and helping to maintain communications in days when land travel was both slow and uncertain, but he was no ornithologist.

He has been credited with a further claim that, following the Tarawera eruption, the White Island gannets

> "Which . . . were formerly so thick upon certain points that you could not stick another gannet in, left the island altogether some time before the eruption and have not returned, and I venture to recommend their unanimity to the notice of the numerous scientists, who will, no doubt, explain in full the why and the wherefore."

In this case he was innocent since the writer was a newspaper correspondent, one of his passengers on a voyage from Wellington to Tauranga in June, 1886. Sladden pointed to the obvious fact that at this particular time of the year the birds are absent from the island in any case, so their departure did not impute to them any abnormal prescience in the sphere of volcanic activity.

When my friends and I began operations we had the results of Stein's meticulous observations to guide us on the timetable of laying, hatching and maturity of chicks. From the ages of the young birds on which we worked it was evident that in both 1959 and 1960 the peak of the laying period occurred between 27 August and 3 September, and the bulk of hatching from 15 to 22 October. While it has been confirmed that a second or even third egg may be laid in one season, such laying only follows the loss of an earlier egg or chick. It is not the normal practice to raise two broods.

If, as Fairchild told of his studies at Gannet Island near Kawhia, both parents sat on eggs in adjoining nests, how would incubation continue during the inevitable absence of at least one bird for feeding? It is true that on a hot day an egg can be seen left unattended for a time, and it may come to no harm, but such weather can hardly be expected to last for six weeks without a break.

Not only Fairchild was led astray by appearances. Even such a careful observer as Sladden believed an extensive white area on the northern benches to mark the site of an abandoned gannetry. This was not accepted by Messrs I.L. Baumgart and E.F. Stokes, who accompanied the 1949 expedition. Small hollows appear in the surface, reminiscent of gannet nests, but the latter would normally be eroded by the weather in a couple of years. The pedologists considered these cavities to have been due to "wind pot-holing", and the white surface covering to be the result of evaporation of salt spray blown ashore during northerly gales.

The paucity of bird life along the northern coast is quite remarkable when contrasted with the teeming abundance of the southern shore during the breeding season. In 1960 Lieut D.J. Broadbent, R.N. took *Mako* slowly along the north side of the island so that our party could look for birds, but our binoculars revealed nothing more than the occasional red-billed gull.

Although the northern gannetry evidently did not exist, two sites which may once have been occupied by breeding birds are now deserted. In 1912 Oliver suggested that nesting gannets were using the Club Rocks. This was, of course, quite possible since the stacks have long served as a roost, though in recent years at least the area has been dominated by the white-fronted terns.

After the concrete dam was built, Sladden noticed gannets were attracted to its vicinity, and estimated their numbers at 100 to 150 birds. The spot was not easy to reach, and this rather vague tally for a comparatively small population suggests that he may not have inspected the site at close quarters. None were there in 1947, and numerous later observations have not recorded any activity in the area.

The present colonies are clustered around three promontories along the south and west coasts, which enjoy at least some measure of shelter on this small exposed island. These are

Otaketake (Gannet Point), Ohauora (Rocky Point) and Te Matawiwi (West Point). The first and last of these are bold headlands reminiscent of Cape Kidnappers. The third is rather strangely an almost flat site only a few feet above the water, an unusual choice since the gannet generally prefers a lofty steep sided area for convenience when flying off.

By far the largest single colony is known as Otaketake "a", occupying much though by no means all of the crest of this wide outlying buttress of the cone. Photographs taken over a number of years show considerable variations in occupancy, and this gannetry illustrates most clearly the puzzling population fluctuations which are a feature of White Island.

Stein's researches have demonstrated that the gannet can live for more than twenty years, returning regularly to its original breeding ground after spending the first few years of life in Australia. It is of course obvious to expect more chicks to be reared in a favourable season than in one when the weather is consistently bad. On the other hand such differences from year to year might be thought to have an effect more marginal than material in view of the necessarily large proportion of comparatively old birds due to the longevity of the species. Chick mortality can be very high, while bands returned from Australia have generally been found on young birds in juvenile plumage which have died near the end of their flight across the Tasman Sea. Many others are doubtless lost too far from land to ever be recovered.

The number of breeding pairs at the colonies were counted both in 1947 and 1949, with the following results:

	Otaketake	Ohauora	Te Matawiwi
1947	2565	1408	1254
1949	2650	1359	1367

It will be seen that the overall total in the latter case was estimated to be 5,376 pairs, or 10,752 birds. This figure did not include the chicks which, with a 97% hatching success, might reach a peak of as many as another 5,000, nor the "unemployed" adults who for one reason or another were not nesting at the time. It is not possible to say how numerous the latter might be.

Since Air Force planes were taking cameras on bombing practice runs over the Volkner Rocks, it seemed to me that here was a splendid chance to get some up-to-date counts, which were quite beyond us on the ground because of our very limited time in the field.

In answer to my application, the Station Commander at Ohakea politely enquired whether oblique photographs taken by low-flying Devon aircraft or vertical pictures from Canberras would be best suited to our purpose. I asked for the latter, and in due course received a set of high definition prints 11½ by 13¼ ins. in size.

When these arrived I was rather busy clearing up my affairs before leaving Whakatane, so Vic kindly took on the job of counting, a rather tedious affair. It involved placing a transparent grid over a photograph, then carefully counting and recording the number of birds and nests in each square. At the cost, as he put it, of a pair of "badly screwed eyeballs," the new set of figures was produced.

The pictures were taken on 12 July 1961, which was a little too early in the year for the colonies to have reached maximum use:

Otaketake	Ohauora	Te Matawiwi
2,326	993	920

The total of 4,239 pairs was well below the earlier counts, but it is very probable that later in the season there could have been as many as another thousand from latecomers.

Some interesting results have emerged from the banding, over a period of years, of about 2,000 gannets. As was expected, the bands recovered showed that the birds normally flew to Australia upon leaving the colonies. It was rare for these migrants to visit Tasmania, only one White Island bird having gone there and two from Horuhoru.

The most distant point reached by a gannet from the Bay of Plenty was Vivonne Bay, on the southern coast of Kangaroo Island, South Australia. It must be remembered that, in order

191

to feed, the bird would have had to travel by way of Bass Strait, so the distance it covered could hardly have been less than 2,000 miles.

The extreme limits of the arc of the Australian coast visited by the birds have so far been Proserpine in North Queensland (latitude 20°25′S.) and Marion Bay, Tasmania (42°53′S.). One quite marked feature of the flights has been the northward trend of the migratory track as time went on.

No bands were returned from Queensland until 1966. Since then the state has rivalled New South Wales as the most popular destination, while the proportion going to Victoria has declined. The gannet has near relatives which spend most of their lives in the tropics.

At one time Stein had doubts about this habitual sojourn of the young birds in Australia. Two boys came upon an immature gannet dead on a west coast beach long after the usual departure season. He made enquiries in his thorough manner, but was unable to trace more than a very small number of birds which had remained in New Zealand. One gannet banded at White Island was later found at the Cape Kidnappers colony. It seems that injury or hatching late in the season account for at least some of these rare exceptions to the general rule.

In the early sixties Vic built himself a surfboat on the lines of those used by rescue crews at Australian beaches. This craft, which he called *Nukutere*, has enabled later parties to stay at White Island for as long as a week at a time, with great benefit to banding and observation work. He has been helped on these visits by his brother Bruce, Brian Doggett, Clifford W. Hawkins, Roy M. Weston and others.

The gannetries are such conspicuous features of the landscape, being visible to the naked eye some twenty-five miles away, that perhaps few people realise the gannet is far outnumbered on the island by the grey-faced petrel, or North Island muttonbird (*Pterodroma macroptera*). A recent official estimate put the total as high as 60,000 plus or minus 5% during the breeding season, from July to January.

The rotary drier has succumbed to corrosion and collapsed

The Fordson tractor disintegrates beneath a fallen roof beam

H.M.N.Z.S. *Mako* lay on her starboard side at the mouth of the Whakatane River as the tide fell

This bird, much smaller than the gannet, is in every way so retiring as to make study of its life cycle very difficult. In the first place it is pelagic, roaming widely over the South Pacific except when it has to use the land to breed. It does not migrate to the Arctic Ocean in the same way as its counterpart the sooty shearwater, or South Island muttonbird (*Puffinus griseus*), which has also been seen at White Island and in isolated cases may breed there.

In addition to spending six months of the year entirely at sea, the grey-faced petrel generally comes ashore to its nest at night. Even when it is seen in coastal waters, perhaps in a fading evening light or very early morning, its dark brown and grey plumage blends into the shadows. Only its strong and rapid flight is at all likely to attract attention.

Rather remarkably, considering that the open ocean is their natural environment, muttonbirds are apt to become confused in stormy weather to an extent which particularly impressed Gilberd. Their practice of laying eggs indiscriminately under the trees seemed to stem from inability to find their own burrows in these conditions. For a time the engineer lived in the guest house, which was some distance from the rest of the camp. If he walked to his quarters without a torch on a rough night he was liable to step on birds laying eggs or roosting on the ground.

The petrels were always liable to collide with overhead electric lines, and had a habit of landing with a thump on the roof of Gilberd's cottage. Once, when comfortably tucked up in bed for the night, he had to get up again to rescue a flapping muttonbird unable to get out of his rainwater cistern. On another occasion a game of chess was ruined because a bird flew in through the open window and scattered the chessmen.

Sladden and Dr R.A. Falla of the Dominion Museum made a survey of various petrels in the Bay of Plenty, and considered the muttonbird did not form colonies in the manner of many seabirds, but was concerned only to find coastal soil of a suitable nature and depth for burrowing. The large number of birds ensured that such a favourable site as the loose ground at White Island would be so heavily populated as to suggest a true

193

colony, but the grey-faced petrel does in fact nest in small concentrations and even singly on the mainland, where it has been largely driven out by the development of land for farming and the inroads of dogs. The pressure on available space at the island is so great that instances have occurred where the very edge of a gannetry has been undermined by muttonbirds.

The burrows can often be of quite considerable size, a tunnel of as much as four feet long leading to the nesting chamber; on occasion several holes may branch off from a single entrance. Falla found sufficient material in one nest to fill half a sugar bag, but this was evidently exceptional, since a lining of only a few dead leaves is more usual.

The single egg, comparatively large for the size of the bird, which is a little larger than the red-billed gull, is laid at the end of July or early in August. As with the gannet, both birds take turns with incubating the egg, most chicks hatching out in September.

The youngster develops an attractive fluffy grey down covering, and grows rapidly in weight until November, when it may weigh more than an adult. Before muttonbirding came to an end at White Island the annual take by hunters over the last ten years averaged between four and five thousand. Those unmolested are fully fledged in January, and leave at the end of the month.

The absence of chicks noted on our early visits to the island was borne out by the 1964 expedition. From virtually none at Otaketake, the number of occupied burrows rose towards the west, reaching a maximum of 15%-20% at Te Matawiwi. This was a marked change from the findings of the 1949 party. In the same month of the year there were then young in most of the burrows opened.

After such a low nesting success for some years one wonders how the very large adult population could be sustained, but banding and other exploratory work on this species is at present in too early a stage to provide reliable information on life expectancy. Ocean birds generally do tend to be long lived, having little to fear from man or other enemies except when breeding.

Once again like the gannet, the fast flying muttonbird is able to find its food at considerable distances from home. It has a marked preference for the octopus family and crustacea, the remains of which have always been found when the stomachs of these birds have been examined.

In addition to the grey-faced petrel and the sooty shearwater, a third seabird nests in burrows at White Island. This is the white-faced storm petrel (*Pelagodroma marina*), though it is present only in small numbers.

On other islands of the Bay of Plenty such as Karewa, Plate and Motoki (one of the Rurima Rocks), the tuatara (*Sphenodon punctatus*) shares quarters with burrowing seabirds. Raymond Buttle believed it lived on White Island, but this is not so. Like so many others, he referred to the creature as merely a lizard, though it is in fact a diminutive leftover from the age of giant reptiles, and looks much like a dinosaur.

Conditions for it on White Island should be quite favourable in view of the absence of dogs and wild pig, with muttonbird burrows for shelter and probably sufficient insects for a food supply. Whether the tuatara was ever here is unknown, but it certainly has not been seen by any expedition during the last twenty years. It might well be worthwhile to introduce a small number of the reptiles, for the more sanctuaries that can be found for it the better chance we have of ensuring its continued survival, which has already lasted since Mesozoic times, thought to be from 65 to 200 million years ago.

Mention has already been made of the places where the sea swallow, or white-fronted tern, is found with the related red-billed gull. Both birds breed on the ground, and so are always much more obvious to the lay observer than the petrels.

By far the most interesting site used by breeding gulls is the beach at Te Awapuia. The birds occupy both sides of the acid stream, the nests gaining some camouflage and protection in such an exposed situation from the big stones and driftwood. The area seems to be an ill-chosen one, for not only is the colony obvious to any chance visitor landing at Crater Bay, but the 1947 expedition saw some nests which were below the

195

level reached by gale-driven seas while others were within nine feet of a steam vent. More recently there has also been hot spring activity here.

The red-billed gull is apt to be transitory in its choice of breeding sites, and the banks of the acid stream have sometimes been found deserted, notably at the time of our early visits. The off-lying rock stacks, however, seem to be regularly used.

The bird has a full measure of the scavenging habits of the *Larus* family to which it belongs. One of those banded at White Island came to grief when feeding in this way. It was following a farmer working the land at Matawhero, near Gisborne, when it came too close to the cultivator and was killed under the discs.

Apart from these seabirds a number of other species, both native and introduced, have been seen at the volcano at one time or another. Some, such as the blackbird (*Turdus merula*) and the house sparrow (*Passer domesticus*) are so common that it would be surprising if they were not present. On the other hand one would hardly expect to find the Arctic skua (*Stercorarius parasiticus*) or the long-tailed cuckoo (*Eudynamis taitensis*), which appear on the list of birds found on or near the island. Many birds are, of course, visitors rather than residents.

Robertson and Weston have both commented recently on an unusual pied fantail (*Rhipidura flabellifera*). This had "no clearly defined brighter plumage and the bird was almost a light muddy grey-brown in colour." There were also irregularities in the tail feathers.

Although Wodzicki's main studies were concentrated upon the gannet, he had the true scientist's curiosity about anything unusual. When at White Island in both 1947 and 1949 he noted the presence of the house sparrow. Bearing in mind the universality of these "mice of the bird world" one might suppose the fact to be of little interest.

This sparrow, as its name suggests, generally lives either in or near human settlements, which readily provide not only food but also both sites and materials for the large untidy nest. Here, on the other hand, the birds were inhabiting a remote island fourteen years after it had been abandoned by man. Two possibilities emerged — these could be progeny of the sparrows then resident, or alternatively be involuntary visitors blown from the mainland by high winds, a fairly common cause of birds appearing in places such as this.

Whatever may have been the origin of this population, it was quite certainly breeding away from human habitation, for nests were located on the cliffs at Troup Head. Wodzicki contributed a paper to the journal of the Royal Australasian Ornithological Union about his find, and in 1954 Messrs Bull and Turbott confirmed a similar occurrence at Great Island in the Three Kings group.

Sladden did not mention the sparrow at White Island during his visits between 1925 and 1927, and Wodzicki asked us to keep a special watch during our new series of field trips. None were seen until 1963, when three birds flew along the cliff face from Ohauora to Crater Bay, possibly making for Troup Head, this being the first recorded sighting since 1949. During the next two years observers saw flocks of up to twenty in this area, and lesser numbers further west.

These records show the house sparrow to resemble the red-billed gull in its variable nesting habits, but unlike the latter it abandons the island altogether for years at a time. The high breeding rate of the species could easily explain the rapid increase in numbers after 1963.

Food would present no problem, since the bird is omnivorous in its feeding habits. Insects are fairly plentiful, and elsewhere sparrows have been seen feeding on the nectar of flax and pohutukawa flowers. There seems to be no real reason why the species should not find an ecological niche here just as it has done over so much of the world.

The volcano has surely demonstrated over the last century that human intruders will gain little from their efforts to despoil it. On the other hand wild creatures seem to be welcome to enjoy the sanctuary which it has to offer from the pressures of modern civilisation.

Is it too much to hope that Whakaari, of such surpassing

interest in so many fields, may one day be linked with other islands in the Bay of Plenty not inhabited by man to form a new national maritime park?

Source Material

40– The Tapsell family connection with the island: (a)
1 *A Trader in Cannibal Land: the life and adventures of Captain Tapsell*, James Cowan. A.H. & A.W. Reed, Wellington 1935; (b) Crown Grant 1. L, Record No. 1GL. 1; (c) Conveyance 2. L, 8 January 1869.

41 *Geology of New Zealand*, Dr Ferdinand von Hochstetter, edited by Dr C.A. Fleming. Wellington, 1959, p. 133.

III *Man Against the Mountain*

43 Title transferred by Conveyance 93454, Record No. R. 18.51.

44 Wellington Exhibition entry, White Island Agricultural Chemical Co. Ltd. sales booklet.

44 Details of bores: *White Island*, Bulletin 127, Department of Scientific & Industrial Research, Wellington 1958. p. 22.

44– Volcanic activity reported: (a) *Wairarapa Standard*,
5 October 1885; (b) *New Zealand Herald*, 23 September 1914.

45 Land transfers: (a) Conveyance 119049, Record No. R. 41.100, 10 October 1891; (b) Conveyance 185237, Record No. R. 135.440, 22 July 1907.

45 Sulphur production, *White Island*, Bulletin, p. 24.

46 Details of New Zealand Sulphur & Fertiliser Co., *New Zealand Herald*, 23 September 1914.

47 *Report on Sulphur Deposits of White Island*, J.L. Stevens.

48– Accidents to firemen: (a) *Auckland Star*, 27 May 1914; (b)
9 *Bay of Plenty Beacon*, 11 February 1952.

50– *Report on the New Zealand Sulphur Company's Property at*
2 *White Island in the Bay of Plenty*, M.F. Mieville, 1914.

53– Staff deaths and sequel, *New Zealand Herald*, September/
6 October 1914.

57 Property bought by A.A. Mercer, Conveyance 326538 Record No. R. 415.619.

58 Capital structure of White Island Agricultural Chemical Co. Ltd., White Island Products Ltd. prospectus, 27 July 1926.

58– Information on White Island (NZ) Sulphur and Fertiliser
9   Co. Ltd., Public Record Office, London, by courtesy of
    Imperial Chemical Industries Ltd. London.

60 T.A. Jaggar (*Volcanoes declare War*) suggested the analogy
    with Krakatoa.

61 Names of radio operators, Norman A. Taylor, 29 October
    1968.

62 Proposed development works outlined in White Island
    Products prospectus.

IV   *White Island Products Ltd.*

66 O.Nicholson to L.M. Eridge, 7 August 1926.

67 G.R. Buttle to Hon Kathleen Vane, 23 October 1926.

72 A.A. Mercer's scheme of arrangement for White Island
    Agricultural Chemical Co. Ltd. was set out in a memoran-
    dum, March 1926.

73 Letters from: (a) A. Davies, 7 July 1926; (b) A. Young,
    22 June 1926; (c) G.L. Ferguson, 10 October 1926.

74 G.R. Buttle to A.Vasey, 3 November 1952.

75– Report to New Zealand Co-operative Dairy Co. Ltd.
6   28 October 1926.

77 G.A. Buttle & Co. to Dymock, MacShane & Sclanders,
    1 October 1926.

78 New Zealand Co-operative Dairy Co.'s decision, G.R.
    Buttle to Hon Kathleen Vane as above.

79 A.A. Mercer to G.R. Buttle, 28 November 1929.

81– Major Miles's work in Australia was reported in letters
2   to G.R. Buttle between February and May, 1927.

82 Possible American interest in White Island Products Ltd.,
    A.A. Mercer to G.R. Buttle, 11 January 1927.

82 Details of White Island (New Zealand) Sulphur, Fertiliser
    and Development Co. Ltd., Public Record Office, London.

83– Robert Kennedy prepared a complete series of reports
6   on the boring programme between 1927–30.

88 Sulphur production, New Zealand Mines Statements,
    1927–8.

89 Ore reserves insufficient, White Island Products Ltd. Annual Report, December 1930.

91 White Island postal history, *Catalogue of New Zealand National Stamp Exhibition, 1967.* Bay of Plenty Philatelic Society, p. 37.

91 Effect of fumes, G.R. Buttle to A. Vasey, 3 November 1952.

93– Life on the island, letter from Mrs H.R. Rosser, 16
6 January 1969.

99 Difficulties of the company, Minutes of Directors' Meeting, 9 March 1931.

100 Shareholders' Meeting, Report by National Bank of New Zealand Ltd., 23 June 1931.

102 Appraisal of sulphur ore reserves, *Report on White Island*
–8 *Sulphur Deposits*, S.J.G. Goosman, 1933.

108 Issue of Debenture, Public Record Office, London.

108 Appointment of Receiver, Liquidation schedules of White Island Products Ltd.

108 Court action in London, *New Zealand Herald*, 20 December
–9 1934.

110 John R. Buttle described his father's purchase of the island.

V   *Conservation Takes Over*

111 G.R. Buttle's comments in this chapter are from his
–19 letter to A. Vasey, 3 November 1952.

112 Dividend payment, Final Report by W.J.A. Thomson, 11 November 1936.

113 Gypsum deposits, J. Healy to G.R. Buttle, 17/28 January 1947.

113 Buttle and Healy's inspection, "Gypsum at White Island," Dr C.A. Fleming, *New Zealand Journal of Science and Technology*, 1948.

114 *Paroto* incident recalled by J.R. Buttle.

116 Island becomes a scenic reserve, *New Zealand Gazette*, 3 December 1953, p. 1448.

117 Muttonbirding prohibited, Secretary for Internal Affairs to J.R. Buttle, 18 July 1968.
118 Aircraft landing, *Helicopter Flight to White Island*, Pro-
–9 fessor R.H. Clark, Wellington, 1968.

VI *Way to the Island*

121 Notes on the Australasian Gannet in this chapter, "Some Observations on the Gannet in Hauraki Gulf," P.A.S. Stein, *Proceedings of the New Zealand Ecological Society*, No. 7, 1960, pp. 38/40.
126 "Te Tahi-o-te-Rangi legend," paper presented to the Whakatane and District Historical Society by the late Albert O. Stewart, 1952.
126 Identification of beaked whale by A.B. Stephenson, Marine Biologist at the Auckland Institute and Museum, 30 June 1969.
127 Paper nautilus washed ashore: (a) *Nature Notes*, Whaka-
–8 tane, July 1958; (b) *White Island — Report of a Survey Expedition 15/24 November 1964*, C.J.R. Robertson, Wellington 1965.
133 Donald Mound temperature, *White Island* Bulletin, p. 35.
137 Chemical reaction over gannetries, *Wanderlust* magazine, T. Crosbie Walsh, 1930, pp. 47/60.
138 Original crater, *White Island* Bulletin, p. 10.
139 Bombing practice, *Daily Post*, Rotorua, 1 March 1961.
140 *New Zealand Herald*, 13 February 1961.

VII *Naval and Legal Occasions*

141 Short-tailed bat discovery, *Journal of the Royal Forest & Bird Protection Society Inc.*, February 1959.
142 H.M.N.Z.S. *Mako* visit, *Bay of Plenty Times*, Tauranga, 14 November 1959.
143 Reconnaissance trip, *Report to the Animal Ecology Section*,
–51 *D.S.I.R.*, 10 September 1960.
151 Gannet poaching case: (a) *Daily Post*, Rotorua, 4 June
–5 1960; (b) *Opotiki News*, 7 June 1960.

153 Death of Captain Stein, "The Development of Ohiwa," Dorothy du Pontet, *Historical Review*, Whakatane, Vol. xi, 1963, p. 122.

156 Loss of the *Aio*, *New Zealand Herald*, 19 November 1967.

162 Supreme Court case, *New Zealand Herald*, 22 August 1963.

VIII *Vulcan's Furnace*

167 *New Zealand: A Narrative* . . ., J.S. Polack, Vol. i, p. 328.
167 Volcanic activity, *New Zealand Herald*, 3 January 1885
–8 and 3 May 1909.
169 Naming of Rudolf vent, Prof. R.H. Clark to J.R. Buttle, 15 February 1968.
169 "On the Crater of White Island," *Transactions of the New Zealand Institute*, Vol. i, pp. 463/5.
170 *White Island*, Dr L.I. Grange. New Zealand Geological Survey Report, 1927.
171 "Notes on the Geology of White Island," Dr J. Hector. *Transactions of the N.Z. Institute* Vol. iii, pp. 278/84.
171 Professor James Park's visit, *New Zealand Herald*, 3 August 1909.
172 *Visit to White Island, 9 February 1968*, J. Healy.
172 Prof. R.H. Clark to J.R. Buttle, 15 February 1968.
173 Gilliver Crater erupts, *Inspection of White Island Crater, 19–20 November 1966*, J. Healy.

IX *Struggle for Existence*

175 "The Vegetation of White Island," Dr W.R.B. Oliver. *Journal of the Linnean Society (Botany)*, London 1915, Vol. 43, p. 41.
175 *Voyage de la Corvette* . . ., Dumont D'Urville.
175 *New Zealand*, Gilbert Mair.
175 *New Zealand: A Narrative* . . ., J.S. Polack, Vol. i, p. 328.
175 "On the Crater of White Island," Edwin and Rolston. *N.Z. Inst. Trans.*, Vol. i, pp. 463/5.

176 "Notes on the Geology . . .," Dr J. Hector. *N.Z. Inst. Trans.*, Vol. iii, p. 279.

176 White Island Products Ltd. prospectus.

176 "He Owns a Volcanic Isle," *Weekly News*, 12 December 1966.

177 Age of pohutukawas, *White Island*, Bulletin, p. 65.

177 Fossil discovery, "Plant Fossils from White Island," Dr C.A. Fleming. "*New Zealand Journal of Geology and Geophysics*," November 1963, Vol. vi, No. 5, pp. 705/6.

178 "The Vegetation of White Island," Dr W.R.B. Oliver, p. 44.

181 *White Island*, Bulletin, pp. 64–5.

X   *"The Meek Shall Inherit . . ."*

187 *A History of the Birds of New Zealand*, Sir Walter Lawry Buller. London 1888, 2nd. ed., Vol. ii, p. 181.

188 Ibid. p. 179.

189 *White Island*, Bulletin, p. 55.

190 Ibid. p. 76.

191 Gannet population, *Report No. 4 to Animal Ecology Division, D.S.I.R. on bird life at White Island, December 1961*, H.D. London. Whakatane, 27 August 1962.

192 Petrel population, P.J. Burstall, Conservator of Wildlife, Rotorua, 6 August 1969.

193 "The Distribution and Breeding Habits of Petrels in
-4 Northern New Zealand," Dr R.A. Falla, *Records of the Auckland Institute & Museum*, 1934 Vol. i (5), p. 255.

196 Unusual pied fantail, C.J.R. Robertson, 3 October 1969.

196 House sparrow on the island: (a) "Breeding of the House
-7 sparrow away from Man in New Zealand," Dr K.A. Wodzicki, *Emu*, Vol. 56, pp. 146/7; (b) *Report to Animal Ecology Division, D.S.I.R. on visits made to White Island on 7/8 December 1963 and 15 February 1964*, R.M. Weston. Kawerau, 30 June 1964.

Index

Index

Index

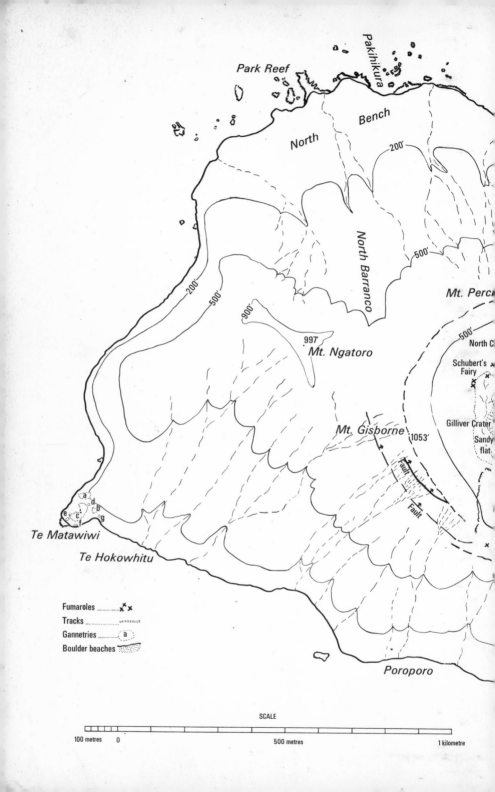

Park Reef

Pakihikura

North Bench

200'

North Barranco

500'

Mt. Perc

200'

500'

900'

997'

Mt. Ngatoro

North C

Schubert's
Fairy

Mt. Gisborne

1053'

Gilliver Crater

Sandy
flat

Fault

Fault

a
d
b
e c g
f

Te Matawiwi

Te Hokowhitu

Poroporo

Fumaroles .... ×ˣ ×
Tracks ....
Gannetries .... a
Boulder beaches

SCALE

100 metres   0   500 metres   1 kilometre